A CENTURY *of*
MANCHESTER

1960s Manchester has always had a multi-cultural society with people from other countries coming to live here. In the nineteenth and early twentieth centuries they came from Europe, often to escape religious persecution. More recently, the cultural mix of Manchester has been enhanced by the arrival of people from places like the West Indies, Africa, the Indian subcontinent and China. This photograph was taken in the late 1960s on Stockport Road, Longsight.

A CENTURY of
MANCHESTER

CHRIS MAKEPEACE

This book was first published in 1999 by Sutton Publishing Limited

This new paperback edition first published in 2007 by Sutton Publishing,

Reprinted in 2009 by
The History Press
The Mill, Brimscombe Port,
Stroud, Gloucestershire, GL5 2QG
www.thehistorypress.co.uk

Reprinted 2010, 2011, 2012

British Library Cataloguing in Publication Data
A catalogue record for this book is available from the British Library.

ISBN 978-0-7509-4917-0

Front endpaper: The offices of the *Manchester Guardian,* 1902.
Back endpaper: Although Manchester can trace its origins back to the Roman occupation of the area,
modern Manchester is the product of the last two and a half centuries. The old market town was
substantially rebuilt in the nineteenth century and many of these buildings have been replaced in the latter
half of the twentieth century. Yet pockets of these earlier buildings remain, such as one side of Market Street
where, facing the Arndale Centre, stand buildings from the nineteenth century. All that is required is for
people to use their eyes and look above shop windows. It is surprising what remains in 1999.
Half title page: These children are waiting for the arrival of the special train which was to take them into the
country, away from the threat posed by German air raids, 1939.
Title page: The bookstall at Victoria station, operated by
W.H. Smith & Son, 1908.

Typeset in Photina.
Typesetting and origination by
Sutton Publishing.
Printed and bound in England.

c. **1910** An elderly gentleman feeds the pigeons
at the base of the Albert Memorial.

Contents

c. **1906** In 1848, Mosley Street Independent Chapel closed and was replaced by the Cavendish Congregational Church on Stretford Road, near All Saints, Chorlton-on-Medlock. The new church, designed by Edward Walters in the Early English style, cost £30,000. The spire, which rose to 171 ft, was visible over a wide area. The church closed in 1969 and was demolished four years later. The building on the right housed Paulden's department store, which had been established by William Paulden in 1865. The store, which was one of the first to have electric lighting in Manchester, was destroyed by fire in 1957, as a result of which the store moved to the former Rylands building on Market Street.

Foreword

I am pleased to have been asked to write the foreword to this book on the great European City of Manchester.

Over the years my predecessors in office have used the terms 'Manchester Goes Forward' or 'Manchester Looks Forward'; nowadays Manchester does both. It is a thriving and enterprising city which has come to terms with the changing economic base of its wealth and has become again the city to which others look for ideas as well as change. From leading the world in the Industrial Revolution it has moved on to become a cultural, media and service orientated-city.

Because of its sporting links with football, cricket, basketball and other sports it has married together these and its own local patriotism to sell Manchester to the world. Just as the changes from cotton to engineering were made by its people so were the recent changes in order to lead us into the next millennium.

Chris Makepeace has again produced a book that is a credit to the city. Manchester is a proud city; its people are proud of their city. It has over the years had men and women from all walks of life who have promoted it throughout the world. Long may it continue!

Tony Burns
Lord Mayor of Manchester

1939 Although the country was at war in November 1939, it did not prevent the public marking the end of the First World War as they had done for almost two decades. The Lord Mayor led the tributes to the fallen, but there were no maroons fired to mark the beginning of the two minutes silence, no march-pasts and no salutes fired. Although the public were not encouraged to gather in large numbers, this photograph shows the crowd which gathered on that Armistice Day in St Peter's Square, each person carrying their gas mask.

Britain: A Century of Change

Children gathered around an early wireless set in the 1920s. The speed and forms of communication were to change dramatically as the century advanced. (*Barnaby's Picture Library*)

The delirious rejoicing at the news of the Relief of Mafeking, during the Boer War in May 1900, is a colourful historical moment. But, in retrospect, the introduction that year of the first motor bus was rather more important, signalling another major adjustment to town life. In the previous 60 years railway stations, post-and-telegraph offices, police and fire stations, gas works and gasometers, new livestock markets and covered markets, schools, churches, football grounds, hospitals and asylums, water pumping stations and sewerage plants had totally altered the urban scene, as the country's population tripled and over 70 per cent were born in or moved to the towns.

When Queen Victoria died in 1901, she was measured for her coffin by her grandson Kaiser Wilhelm, the London prostitutes put on black mourning and the blinds came down in the villas and terraces spreading out from the old town centres. These centres were reachable by train and tram, by the new bicycles and still newer motor cars, con-nected by the new telephone, and lit by gas or even electricity. The shops may have been full of British-made cotton and woollen clothing but the grocers and butchers were selling cheap Danish bacon, Argentinian beef, Australasian mutton, tinned or dried fish and fruit from Canada, California and South Africa. Most of these goods were carried in British-built-and-crewed ships, burning Welsh steam coal.

Women working as porters on the Great Western Railway, Paddington, c. 1917. (*W.L. Kenning/ Adrian Vaughan Collection*)

As the first decade moved on, the Open Spaces Act meant more parks, bowling greens and cricket pitches. The first state pensions came in, together with higher taxation and death duties. These were raised mostly to pay for the new Dreadnought battleships needed to maintain naval superiority over Germany, and deter them from war. But the deterrent did not work. The First World War transformed the place of women, as they took over many men's jobs. Its other legacies were the war memorials which joined the statues of Victorian worthies in main squares round the land. After 1918 death duties bit even harder and a quarter of England changed hands in a few years.

The multiple shop – the chain store – appeared in the high street: Sainsburys, Maypole, Lipton's, Home & Colonial, the Fifty Shilling Tailor, Burton, Boots, W.H. Smith. The shopper was spoilt for choice, attracted by the brash fascias and advertising hoardings for national brands like

Bovril, Pears Soap, and Ovaltine. Many new buildings began to be seen, such as garages, motor showrooms, picture palaces (cinemas), 'palais de dance', and the bow-windowed, pebble-dashed, tile-hung, half-timbered houses that were built as ribbon-development along the roads and new bypasses or on the new estates nudging the green belts.

During the 1920s cars became more reliable and sophisticated as well as commonplace, with developments like the electric self-starter making them easier for women to drive. Who wanted to turn a crank handle in the new short skirt? This was, indeed, the electric age as much as the motor era. Trolley buses, electric trams and trains extended mass transport and electric light replaced gas in the street and the home, which itself was groomed by the vacuum cleaner.

A major jolt to the march onward and upward was administered by the Great Depression of the early 1930s. The older British industries – textiles, shipbuilding, iron, steel, coal – were already under pressure from foreign competition when this worldwide slump arrived, cutting exports by half in two years and producing 3 million unemployed (and still rising) by 1932. Luckily there were new diversions to alleviate the misery. The 'talkies' arrived in the cinemas; more and more radios and gramophones were to be found in people's homes; there were new women's magazines, with fashion, cookery tips and problem pages; football pools; the flying feats of women pilots like Amy Johnson; the Loch Ness Monster; cheap chocolate and the drama of Edward VIII's abdication.

Father and child cycling past Buckingham Palace on VE Day, 8 May 1945. (*Hulton Getty Picture Collection*)

Things were looking up again by 1936 and unemployment was down to 2 million. New light industry was booming in the Home Counties as factories struggled to keep up with the demand for radios, radiograms, cars and electronic goods including the first television sets. The threat from Hitler's Germany meant rearmament, particularly of the airforce, which stimulated aircraft and aero engine firms. If you were lucky and lived in the south, there was good money to be earned. A semi-detached house cost £450, a Morris Cowley £150. People may have smoked like chimneys but life expectancy, since 1918, was up by 15 years while the birth rate had almost halved. The fifty-four hour week was down to forty-eight hours and there were 9 million radio licences by 1939.

In some ways it is the little memories that seem to linger longest from the Second World War: the kerbs painted white to show up in the blackout, the rattle of ack-ack shrapnel on roof tiles, sparrows killed by

A family gathered around their television set in the 1950s. (*Hulton Getty Picture Collection*)

bomb blast, painting your legs brown and then adding a black seam down the back to simulate stockings. The biggest damage, apart from London, was in the south-west (Plymouth, Bristol) and the Midlands (Coventry, Birmingham). Postwar reconstruction was rooted in the Beveridge Report which set out the expectations for the Welfare State. This, together with the nationalisation of the Bank of England, coal, gas, electricity and the railways, formed the programme of the Labour government in 1945. At this time the USA was calling in its debts and Britain was beggared by the war, yet still administering its Empire.

Times were hard in the late 1940s, with rationing even more stringent than during the war. Yet this was, as has been said, 'an innocent and well-behaved era'. The first let-up came in 1951 with the Festival of Britain and then there was another fillip in 1953 from the Coronation, which incidentally gave a huge boost to the spread of TV. By 1954 leisure motoring had been resumed but the Comet – Britain's best hope for taking on the American aviation industry – suffered a series of mysterious crashes. The Suez debacle of 1956 was followed by an acceleration in the withdrawal from Empire, which had begun in 1947 with the Independence of India. Consumerism was truly born with the advent of commercial TV and most homes soon boasted washing machines, fridges, electric irons and fires.

The *Lady Chatterley* obscenity trial in 1960 was something of a straw in the wind for what was to follow in that decade. A collective loss of inhibition seemed to sweep the land, as stately home owners opened up, the Beatles and the Rolling Stones transformed popular music, and retailing, cinema and the theatre were revolutionised. Designers, hairdressers, photographers and models moved into places vacated by an Establishment put to flight by the new breed of satirists spawned by *Beyond the Fringe* and *Private Eye*.

In the 1970s Britain seems to have suffered a prolonged hangover after the excesses of the previous decade. Ulster, inflation and union troubles were not made up for by entry into the EEC, North Sea Oil, Women's Lib or, indeed, Punk Rock. Mrs Thatcher applied the corrective in the 1980s, as the country moved more and more from its old manufacturing base over to providing services, consulting, advertising, and expertise in the 'invisible' market of high finance or in IT. Britain entertained the world with *Cats*, *Phantom of the Opera*, *Four Weddings and a Funeral*, *The Full Monty*, *Mr Bean* and the *Teletubbies*.

The post-1945 townscape has seen changes to match those in the worlds of work, entertainment and politics. In 1956 the Clean Air Act served notice on smogs and pea-souper fogs, smuts and blackened buildings, forcing people to stop burning coal and go over to smokeless sources of heat and energy. In the same decade some of the best urban building took place in the 'new towns' like Basildon, Crawley, Stevenage and Harlow. Elsewhere open warfare was declared on slums and what was labelled inadequate, cramped, back-to-back, two-up, two-down, housing. The new 'machine for living in' was a flat in a high-rise block. The architects and planners who promoted these were in league

Carnaby Street in the 1960s. (*Barnaby's Picture Library*)

13

The Millennium Dome at Greenwich, 1999. (*Michael Durnan/ Barnaby's Picture Library*)

with the traffic engineers, determined to keep the motor car moving whatever the price in multi-storey car parks, meters, traffic wardens and ring roads.

The old pollutant, coal smoke, was replaced by petrol and diesel exhaust, and traffic noise. Even in the back garden it was hard to find peace as motor mowers, then leaf blowers and strimmers made themselves heard, and the neighbours let you share their choice of music from their powerful new amplifiers, whether you wanted to or not. Fast food was no longer only a pork pie in a pub or fish-and-chips. There were Indian curry houses, Chinese take-aways and American-style hamburgers, while the drinker could get away from beer in a wine bar. Under the impact of television the big Gaumonts and Odeons closed or were rebuilt as multi-screen cinemas, while the palais de dance gave way to discos and clubs.

From the late 1960s the introduction of listed buildings and conservation areas, together with the growth of preservation societies, put a brake on 'comprehensive redevelopment'. Now the new risk at the end of the 1990s is that town centres may die, as shoppers are attracted to the edge-of-town supermarkets surrounded by parking space, where much more than food and groceries can be bought. The ease of the one-stop shop represents the latest challenge to the good health of our towns. But with care, ingenuity and a determination to keep control of our environment, this challenge can be met.

Manchester: An Introduction

Although Manchester can trace its history back to the Roman fort at Castlefield, it is only in the last 250 years that the city has grown in size and importance, making a significant contribution to the British economy as well as the development of a social conscience. Manchester's success was based on commerce and trade, symbolised by the Free Trade Hall, which A.J.P. Taylor pointed out was the only public hall named after an economic concept. The importance of trade and commerce in the economic and social life of Manchester was noted by Professor G.W. Daniels in 1929 when he wrote, in the foreword to *Manchester at Work* that 'Few communities have a livelier sense of local patriotism: but the mere size of the city makes it impossible for the citizen, unaided, to take in and realise the scale and variety of social activities of which it is the scene or centre. For many people, Manchester means cotton (which incidentally was the same comment with which *Picture Post* opened an article on Manchester in November 1938); for a smaller, but nevertheless large and world-wide clientele, it stands for electrical equipment, locomotives, raincoats and a hundred other industrial products. Its reputation is no less widespread as the home of a great political tradition . . .'.

A few years later, in 1934, the anonymous author of an article published in *Manchester Goes Forward* commented that 'A city goes forward under the impetus of two fundamental influences – its resources and its man-power. These are the raw materials for progress, the city advancing by the full development of its resources under the inspiration of its citizens . . . Manchester – one of the great commercial centres of the world – is built on the immortal work of her citizens . . . Manchester goes forward looking a well-managed city . . . applying itself with determination to correcting errors of the past and planning for the future with foresight and courage.' He was saying that Manchester was a forward-looking city and should not apologise for this as this quality had made the city great in the past and would do so again in the future.

In 1945, the Lord Mayor, speaking to the crowds in Albert Square on VJ Day, commented that 'We in Manchester look forward with hope and confidence'. The Council faced big challenges in the immediate postwar period, but they had for guidance *The Manchester Plan 1945*, prepared by the City Surveyor and Engineer, which outlined how the city ought to develop in the last half of the twentieth century. This was the first of many plans for the development of Manchester that have been produced, the most recent being for the area around the Market Place, devastated by an IRA bomb in 1996. Increasingly, the public have been given the opportunity to comment on these plans and their comments are listened to and some are incorporated.

Looking back, the twentieth century has been a period of change. Although change has taken place in other centuries as well, one difference between this and the nineteenth century is that people are more aware of change and are prepared to voice their opinions on it far more than in the past. It also takes place faster than it did a century ago.

During the twentieth century, Manchester's boundaries have moved. In 1904 Withington Urban District Council was absorbed and, in 1931, a large part of north Cheshire was taken over to become the Wythenshawe estate. Manchester's population peaked in 1931 at 766,333 as a result of these boundary changes but the growth in the physical size of Manchester masked the fact the people were moving out to more pleasant, semi-rural areas – a trend which also existed in the nineteenth century when merchants and businessmen moved to places like Victoria Park and Didsbury. The gradual fall in Manchester's population was also helped by the slum clearance programmes of the postwar era when overspill estates were set up to rehouse those displaced by the demolition of the densely populated areas like Hulme and Chorlton-on-Medlock.

Change has also affected the way people travel. The motor car has replaced the bus, tram and train as a means of getting to work, to the shops and to leisure activities. Attempts are made to encourage people to use public transport and the reintroduction of the trams is a step in this direction.

The growth in the use of the private car has led to other challenges. For instance, the increasing number of out-of-town shopping areas, like the Trafford Centre, has posed a serious threat to the shops of central Manchester but they appear to be meeting the challenge and attracting people into central Manchester to shop. Once the redevelopment resulting from the IRA bomb blast is complete, central Manchester and its shops will be in a far better position to compete than they were before.

Industry has also changed in the twentieth century. Gone are the old, dirty heavy industries, such as engineering and steel-making, while the cotton industry has also disappeared, both in terms of the

manufacturing side where Manchester was not strong but also the commercial side with its warehouses. In their place new high-tech industries and service industries have grown up, many of which are based on tourism and leisure. With the changes in industry and commerce have come changes in the use of buildings. Some buildings are capable of adaptation to new uses but others are not. For instance, Watts Warehouse has been converted into a hotel and the former Central station into an exhibition centre. The question which has to be resolved is which buildings should remain and which should go. It is not possible to keep everything and, for those which are to be retained, a viable use has to be found.

At the beginning of the twentieth century, Manchester meant cotton. Today, if the name 'Manchester' is mentioned, people recognise the city as the home of Manchester United football club or the location of a long-running soap opera on television – *Coronation Street*. However,

c. **1935** A newspaper vendor sits in the sun on the wall surrounding Piccadilly Gardens and reads one of the papers or magazines she has in stock. Her location would have been a good one as not only was the bus station nearby, but many people would have passed the stand on their way to and from London Road station.

17

1938 In June 1938 George VI visited Manchester to open the Town Hall Extension. Large crowds turned out for his first visit to Manchester as king. This photograph shows the corner of Princess Street and Albert Square with some of the decorations which were put up for the visit together with the canopy erected at the main entrance to the Town Hall. The new building not only provided additional offices for the staff of the City Council, but also a new Council Chamber, which was very much needed as the number of councillors and aldermen had increased as a result of Manchester's growth in size between 1885 and 1931.

Manchester is far more than either of these – it is a vibrant city that is playing its traditional role as a leader both locally, regionally, nationally and, now, internationally. Manchester is in an excellent position to strengthen this role during the twenty-first century. The words written in 1934 hold true today as much as they did when they were first written over 60 years ago and likewise, the Lord Mayor's comments of VJ Day also hold true.

The Beginning of the Century

c. **1912**   An early morning scene on the boundaries of Manchester and Chorlton-on-Medlock as the milk is delivered to a shop possibly on the corner of Charles Street and York Street. The houses on the left, still occupied when the photograph was taken, were built in the early nineteenth century as back-to-back properties with cellars underneath, but whether they had been converted into ordinary houses by this time is not certain. The building between the houses and the viaduct carrying the railway between London Road and Oxford Road stations was built in the mid-nineteenth century and used as a workshop. In the background is Paul Waterhouse's extension to the Refuge Assurance Company's building, completed in 1912.

1901   Although Queen Victoria's death was expected, when the news was received it still sent shock waves through the community. The local newspapers devoted many column inches to her life and reign, including her three visits to Manchester in 1851, 1857 and 1894. The official proclamation announcing her death and the accession of Edward VII was read by the Lord Mayor, Alderman Thomas Briggs, accompanied by members of the council, from the steps of the Town Hall. It was the first time in Manchester's history that there had been a mayor to proclaim a new monarch because, when Victoria came to the throne in 1837, Manchester was not a borough. Immediately after the proclamation had been read, the Union Jack was raised, and then lowered to half-mast.

1901   To mark Victoria's Diamond Jubilee in 1897, Manchester commissioned Onslow Ford to create a statue of her to be paid for by public subscription and erected in the centre of the Esplanade in Piccadilly. The new statue was unveiled by Field Marshal Lord Roberts on 10 October, exactly 50 years to the day of Queen Victoria's first visit to Manchester. The ceremony was attended by a huge crowd, who used every vantage-point to watch the proceedings. So dense was the throng that some of the guests in a grandstand were forced to climb over the railings surrounding the Infirmary to get away from the crush.

1905 On 13 July, the Manchester Ship Canal Company's new No. 9 dock, built on the site of the former Manchester Race Course, was officially opened by Edward VII and Queen Alexandra. Having opened the new dock, the king undertook other official engagements in Salford. Here is the royal procession in Piccadilly passing the statue of Queen Victoria. In the background is the Royal Hotel, on the corner of Mosley Street and Piccadilly, which was demolished in 1908.

1909 In December 1908, the Manchester Royal Infirmary completed the move from its old buildings in Piccadilly to its new premises in Chorlton-on-Medlock. The new hospital building was officially opened by Edward VII and Queen Alexandra on 6 July 1909, and afterwards the king and queen toured the hospital and named two wards, the King Edward VII Ward and the Queen Alexandra Ward. Here they are leaving the Infirmary to drive along streets lined with enthusiastic Mancunians.

1911 On 27 April, members attending the Royal Exchange suspended business and sang the National Anthem to mark the coronation of George V. How many members were present on this occasion is not known, but the photograph shows a very crowded floor. In 1913, the membership of the Royal Exchange exceeded 13,000, of which about half regularly attended on Tuesday and Thursday afternoons, which were known as 'High 'Change', making the area around the building one of constant activity.

1913 On 14 July, George V visited Manchester for the first time as reigning monarch. After being welcomed at London Road station, the king and queen travelled in an open carriage to Platt Fields, where they were greeted by a large gathering of Manchester schoolchildren. Afterwards, the royal party returned to central Manchester where the king knighted the Lord Mayor, Alderman Samuel Royse, in front of the large crowd assembled in Albert Square.

1910 Manchester Victoria station, built by the Manchester & Leeds Railway (later the Lancashire & Yorkshire Railway) to replace its station on Oldham Road, was opened in 1844. Until 1884, the station was shared with the London & North Western Railway when this company moved to Exchange Station. During the nineteenth century, the station was enlarged on several occasions so that by 1910, it had seventeen platforms and handled almost 100,000 passengers each day. This is the office building which was added during the final phase of expansion in the early twentieth century with the canopy over the pavement listing some of the towns served by the company.

c. **1903**   Although in Salford, Exchange station was always known as 'Manchester Exchange'. It was built by the London & North Western Railway Company in 1884 when the company was becoming concerned that it might be forced to leave Victoria station as that station was being constantly enlarged to meet the growing level of traffic. This is the approach to the station from Victoria Street, across the River Irwell. In the centre is the statue of Oliver Cromwell, which was given to Manchester by Mrs Abel Heywood in memory of her first husband, Alderman Goadsby, in 1877. When it was unveiled, it was the first full-sized statue of Cromwell in the country. Exchange station was closed in 1969 and the site used as a car park.

c. **1910**   London Road station, now Piccadilly station, was opened by the Manchester & Birmingham Railway in 1842 to replace a temporary station which had been opened in 1840. In the early days, the station was approached by a flight of stairs from Store Street, but later an inclined road was constructed to provide access for road vehicles to the station. The station was jointly used by the London & North Western Railway and the Manchester Sheffield & Lincolnshire Railway, although relations were far from smooth. The station buildings shown here were erected in the mid-1860s, while the train shed was enlarged at the end of the century.

1913 When Central station, owned by the Cheshire Lines Committee, was opened in 1880, it was the main line station that was closest to the centre of Manchester. The main feature of the station was the 210-ft span of the train shed arch, which was always clearly visible as the office block and hotel proposed for the front of the station was never constructed. When the Midland Hotel was built on a adjacent site, it was linked to the station by a covered way which can be seen in the photograph. During its heyday in the early twentieth century, the company's services to places like London and Liverpool received high praise for their punctuality and efficiency.

c. **1907** One of the companies that used Central station was the Midland Railway. In 1898, the company purchased a site bounded by Lower Mosley Street, Peter Street, Mount Street and Windmill Street, demolished the buildings and erected a prestigious new hotel. Known as the Midland, it was opened in 1904 and had all the latest conveniences including electricity, passenger lifts and roof garden. This is the front of the building overlooking Peter Street and St Peter's Square. On the right are the buildings which were demolished in the late 1920s to make way for the new Central Library.

1907 One of the most famous meetings ever to take place in Manchester was held at the Midland Hotel in 1904 when the Hon. Charles Rolls met Frederick Royce (inset), a Manchester electrical engineer with an interest in cars. The result was the formation of Rolls-Royce Cars. The new cars were manufactured in Manchester until the firm moved to Derby in 1907. This Rolls-Royce, known later as the 'Pearl of the East' was originally owned by Frank Norbury, a colour and ticket printer of Old Trafford. The car had a 40/50hp 6-cylinder engine with a body by the Manchester firm of Joseph Cockshoot. Norbury sold his business in 1907 and went to India with the car where it was shown at the Bombay Motor Show and took part in long-distance reliability trials.

1901 When horse trams were introduced in 1878, the track had been laid by Manchester Corporation and leased to individual operators for 20 years. When the leases came up for renewal, the city decided to electrify the system and run the trams itself. By June 1901, the first route was ready to operate and work was progressing on extending the network. The opening of the electrified system took place on 6 June 1901 with the first electric tram to run between Manchester (Albert Square) and Cheetham Hill being driven by the Lord Mayor.

c. **1902** Although electric trams were introduced in 1901, it took several years before all the horse tram routes were converted to the new form of traction. This photograph, taken in Piccadilly about 1902, shows horse trams were still operating to Old Trafford and Belle Vue. The route between Piccadilly and Old Trafford was converted to electric traction in March 1903 and became route 27. It is possible that the Belle Vue tram may have been en route to Victoria Street. This particular tram route became the 34/34A service and was electrified in June 1902, although it is possible that horse-drawn trams were used at busy periods to cope with the traffic to Belle Vue.

1910 On 28 April, Louis Paulham, a Frenchman, flying a Farman biplane, completed the first flight between London and Manchester to win a prize of £10,000 offered by the *Daily Mail*. Paulham left Hendon on the evening of 27 April, closely pursued by an Englishman, Claude Grahame-White, who took off from Wormwood Scrubs an hour after Paulham. When darkness fell, both pilots had to land, but although Grahame-White took off again from Roade in Northamptonshire very early in the morning, bad weather forced him to retire. Paulham landed at Lichfield when it became too dark to fly, but as soon as it was light enough took off and, following the railway past Crewe and Sandbach, landed in a field near Burnage station at 5.32 a.m., where he was greeted by a large crowd.

1907 As the motor car gained popularity, several firms were established in the Manchester area making car engines and chassis. One of these was Horsfall and Bickham, established engineers in Salford. Their first cars were produced in 1902 with bodies by Manchester's leading coachbuilders, Joseph Cockshoot and Anne Cowburn. The *Motor Car Journal* reported that 'these machines are extremely well built and are finished on engineering lines'. Here is a 20hp model with two unknown, but suitably dressed, ladies on board.

1902 When John Owens died in 1846, he left almost £100,000 to establish an institution of higher education which did not require those wishing to attend or teach there to undergo any form of religious test. The new college, named Owens College, was opened in 1851 in premises on Quay Street, where it remained until 1873 when it moved to a 4-acre site in Chorlton-on-Medlock. Gradually, the number of buildings increased to meet the growing number of students and the increasing range of subjects taught. In 1902, the Whitworth Hall, shown here, was completed and opened by the Prince and Princess of Wales. Since 1902, the University of Manchester has continued to expand and now covers an extensive area along Oxford Road.

c. **1913** During the nineteenth century, Manchester Literary and Philosophical Society played a major role in enabling scientists like John Dalton and J.P. Joule to report on their work and in disseminating the information to other scientists. This role continued into the early twentieth century when scientists like Ernest Rutherford and Neils Bohr, shown here with their wives, made significant advances in the field of nuclear physics. It was Rutherford, Professor of Physics at Manchester University, who made the first and only major modification to Dalton's Atomic Theory, put forward in 1812. Rutherford spoke from the same platform as Dalton had used and at a meeting of the same society, the Manchester Literary and Philosophical Society. Rutherford was elected a member of the Lit & Phil in 1907 and Bohr was elected an honorary member in 1914.

1909 For over 150 years, Piccadilly was dominated by the Manchester Royal Infirmary. The Infirmary had been founded in 1752 and had moved to Piccadilly in 1755, gradually enlarging the building it occupied until by the beginning of the twentieth century it was not able to expand any more, having over 270 beds, which were occupied nearly all the time. As medical treatments improved and new diagnostic techniques were introduced, the old buildings became increasingly inadequate, so the decision was taken in 1902 to move to a new site on Nelson Street. The move took place at the end of 1908 and the old building was demolished early in 1910. This photograph, possibly taken in 1909 when Edward VII visited Manchester to open the new hospital, shows the Portland Street façade, which had been incorporated into the main buildings in the mid-nineteenth century when the Lunatic Hospital moved to Cheadle.

29

1914 Traffic congestion has always been a problem in Manchester, so much so that early in the twentieth century the City Engineer's Department undertook a study of the problem and came up with recommendations to try and alleviate it, including the pedestrianisation of Market Street. This photograph shows the junction of Cross Street, Market Street and Corporation Street with horse-drawn vehicles, motor vehicles and trams all jostling for road space while a policeman stands and watches the traffic. Matters were made worse by the fact that this was also a busy pedestrian junction with the Royal Exchange close by.

1914 Although Manchester is associated with the cotton industry, the city's importance lay in the fact that many firms established large warehouses in the town where the products of the various mills could be seen. Many of the warehouses were located between Mosley Street, York Street, Oxford Street and the River Medlock. These tall buildings often gave the streets the appearance of a canyon. They tended to be gloomy and always very busy. This photograph shows the junction of Portland Street and Princess Street with the warehouses on Princess Street dominating the scene.

c. **1910** In the days before radio and television, street entertainment was an important part of everyday life. The arrival of street entertainers provided a welcome break in the daily routine and attracted a crowd of onlookers, as this photograph of a dancing bear in the Shudehill area shows. The bears, often called Bruin, usually came from Russia and were accompanied by a handler who would encourage the bear to take a few lumbering steps before going through the crowd with a bowl collecting donations. With the outbreak of the First World War, dancing bears disappeared from the street scene.

1910 On 7 May, Cllr Charles Behrens, Lord Mayor of Manchester, presided over a ceremony to mark the completion of the conversion of the Platt Fields estate into a public park covering over 80 acres. The opening of the park was the culmination of a campaign, led by William Royle of Rusholme, to prevent the land being used for housing and retain it as a public open space after it had been put on the market by its owners, the Worsley family. The new park included a 6.5-acre lake as well as 3.5 miles of walks, tennis courts and other games facilities.

1911 On 2 September, the 21st Derby match between Manchester City and Manchester United was played at City's Hyde Road ground. This was the first match of the new Football League season when both clubs were in the First Division. The match ended in a 0–0 draw. At the end of the season, Manchester City were 15th and Manchester United were 13th in the league.

1901 The Manchester Volunteers were officially welcomed home from active service in South Africa on 24 May. The day began with a parade at Ashton Barracks, where each man was given a £5 bounty, after which they travelled to Manchester, where they were welcomed by the Lord Mayor and senior officers. The troops then marched from London Road station to the cathedral for a service of thanksgiving before being entertained to lunch by the Lord Mayor in the Town Hall. The appearance of the men was described as being 'grave, soldier like, thin and ill looking' while the procession was 'disappointingly short and had practically nothing of that bright colour which all healthy Englishmen like to see in their pageants'.

c. **1905** Whit Walks have been a feature of Manchester since the nineteenth century with the Sunday schools associated with the Church of England originally walking on Whit Monday and those of the Catholics on the following Friday. For the event, children would have had new clothes and their pictures taken before walking in the procession. The Church of England procession originally started in St Ann's Square, but in 1878 it was moved to the larger Albert Square. In 1901, it was reported that 25,661 children representing 45 churches took part in the Whit Monday procession. This picture shows the C. of E. Whit Walk at the junction of Princess Street and Mosley Street with adult members of the church preceding the Sunday school scholars.

1907 In October 1903, Emmeline Pankhurst called a meeting at her home, 62 Nelson Street, to discuss the growing demand from women to have a greater say in the government of the country through the ballot box. The meeting resulted in the formation of the Women's Social and Political Union, which eventually established its headquarters in London where it undertook political lobbying as well as more direct action to draw attention to its demands. In 1906, an attempt was made to disrupt a meeting at the Free Trade Hall at which the main speaker was Sir Edward Grey, the Foreign Secretary. In the scuffles which followed, a banner was torn down, leaving only the words 'Votes for Women' visible, which began the suffragettes' slogan. This suffragette rally took place in the St James's Theatre on Oxford Street on 6 January.

***c.* 1904** As the population of Manchester grew in the late eighteenth and early nineteenth centuries, houses were erected as quickly as possible with little regard for the well-being of the future residents. Most lacked adequate sanitary facilities with many being built as back-to-back houses or courts. After 1844, the construction of back-to-back houses in Manchester was prohibited as all new property had to have ashpits or privies in a small back yard. However, there was a legacy of earlier houses to be tackled, a problem which was not faced until after 1919. This particular photograph shows houses built round a courtyard, which provided a communal area for the residents to hang out their washing and where the children could play.

***c.* 1903** Early in the century, most towns had at least one brewery and many had several. Today, the number of small independent breweries has declined considerably and few remain. One such is Hydes' Anvil Brewery, which was established in the mid-nineteenth century in Audenshawe, but later moved to Manchester, where it had a brewery near London Road station. It finally moved to its present premises in Moss Side in 1899. These men are working in the bottling department and appear to be bottling and labelling Bass's rather than the company's own beer. Once the beer had been bottled, it took 4 or 5 weeks for it to mature, during which time it was stacked on duckboards to condition it. The whole operation at that time was very labour-intensive as all operations were done by men rather than by machine.

1911 During the years 1911–12 there was much industrial unrest with strikes affecting many aspects of industry and commerce. In summer 1911, Manchester was affected by strikes which involved railway workers, tramways employees and carters. One of the most serious was the carters' strike which threatened food supplies to the city. Both police and troops were used to ensure that those carters who wanted to work could do so without the threat of intimidation and, where necessary, to ensure food supplies reached the markets and were distributed to shops. Here police escort a carter along Newton Street towards Great Ancoats Street.

The First World War

1914 Many methods were tried to encourage men to enlist in the army once the initial enthusiasm of August 1914 had died away. Possibly best known was the recruiting poster which showed the face of Field Marshal Kitchener with the slogan 'Your Country Needs You', a copy of which is at the bottom of the thermometer. A large thermometer was erected in front of Manchester Town Hall which showed how many men were required and how many had volunteered by a particular time. The photograph may have been taken in late August or early September 1914 and gives the target of 1,070 men. To the left, there is another poster for the 15th Battalion Manchester Regiment and one on the ground awaiting erection.

1914 When war broke out in August 1914, the British Army was small compared with those of the continental powers, but it was soon apparent that it would be necessary to increase its size considerably. In order to encourage recruitment, it was suggested at the end of August that special battalions be formed whereby men who worked together would serve in the army together. This resulted in the formation of the so-called 'Pals' battalions. On 1 September 1914, the first battalion of 'Manchester Pals' was formed consisting of 800 men who became the 16th Battalion, Manchester Regiment. Three further battalions were raised in the following weeks. The men reported to Platt Fields and were then transferred to Heaton Park for initial training. The recruits are lined up before leaving for their training camp in autumn 1914.

1914 When the men were first given a uniform, it was blue and very similar to that worn by the guards on Manchester Corporation trams. This displeased the men who felt that they should have been given khaki uniforms, but in 1914 and early 1915 there was a shortage of khaki cloth as the government had requisitioned all stocks for those who were fighting on the front. This photograph shows the uniform of the men, who appear to be learning how to construct a trench and make it safe from collapse.

1915 These men may be returning from a training march in the Heaton Park area. Such marches would have been an essential part of the volunteers' training to ensure that they were at peak fitness when they left for the front. Some of the men look rather tired and do not appear to to be carrying their weapons in the correct manner or even carrying packs on their backs.

1915 By 1915, those men who had volunteered to serve in the Manchester 'Pals' battalions the previous autumn were regarded as having completed their preliminary training and were ordered first to Grantham from where the 15th Battalion was transferred to the front line in France. The 16th battalion was sent to Salisbury Plain to complete its training before being sent to Gallipoli. The men are in Piccadilly, resting after their march from Heaton Park, before moving off to the station.

1914 When the 'Pals' battalions were established in 1914, there was a lack of men to train the raw recruits so retired soldiers, especially non-commissioned officers, were recruited. Likewise, as the men were living under canvas, there was a shortage of men who knew the basics of camping such as how to pitch a tent correctly. As a result, those recruits who had experience of living under canvas, for example former scouts, were often put in charge of tents, which could result in rather awkward situations where an office junior was senior in military terms to his superior at work. This is part of the tented encampment at Heaton Park before the wooden huts, which were more suitable in winter, had been erected. Although the men in the foreground appear to be enjoying themselves, in the background other recruits are undergoing training.

1915 On 21 March 1915, the British Commander-in-Chief, Lord Kitchener, visited Manchester and inspected 11,000 men drawn from the locally raised Manchester 'Pals' Battalions, men from the Manchester Brigade based at Morecambe, detachments from the Lancashire Fusiliers and men from the Bantam Battalions formed in Bury and Chadderton. Kitchener took the salute on a platform in front of the Town Hall, where he was accompanied by other senior officers and the Lord Mayor of Manchester, Daniel McCabe, and the mayors of the other towns whose men were on parade that day. Behind the marching men is another recruitment poster, for the County Palatine Engineers, which were being raised by Lord Derby, and which was seeking men from various occupations for its ranks.

1916 During the First World War, the YMCA took an active role in providing recreational facilities for troops both at home and overseas. In Manchester, permission was granted to erect several huts in Piccadilly on the site of the former Infirmary, so that troops who were at home on leave or who were convalescing from their wounds had somewhere to go, as their wives might have been away during the day at work. The huts were completed late in 1916 and were known as the Manchester YMCA Khaki Club and Hostel.

1916 This picture shows the interior of one of the YMCA Khaki Club huts in Piccadilly. Not only did it provide drinks, such as coffee, tea, cocoa, Horlicks and soft drinks, and food, such as sandwiches and cakes, but also entertainment. There was a stage and piano and it was reported that once the facilities opened, there was no shortage of local groups of musicians and entertainers who were prepared to entertain the men during the evening. In addition, there were also facilities for games – even a billiard table was provided. Every attempt was made to create a homely atmosphere. There was even a large, domestic-type fireplace, which probably provided heating for the room as well.

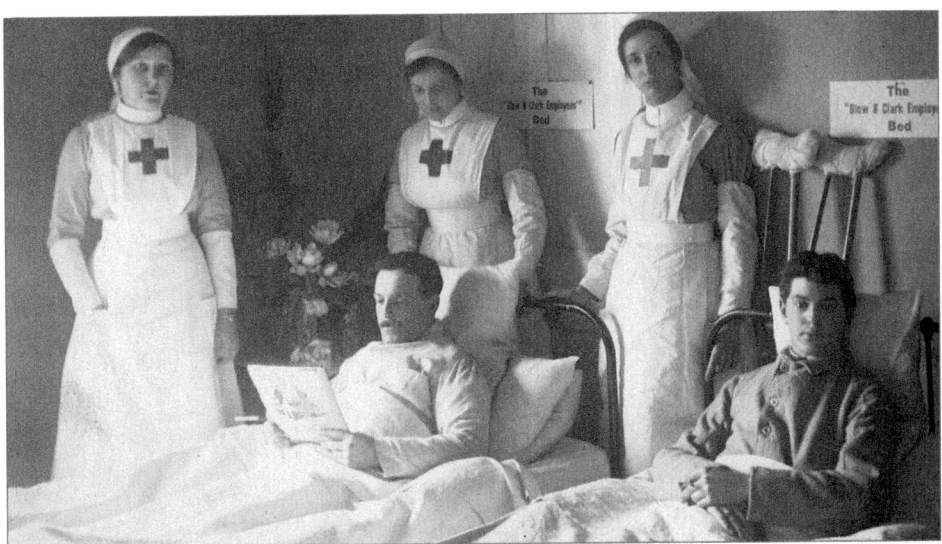

***c.* 1918** In 1916, the British Red Cross Society took over Grangethorpe, a former merchant's house in Fallowfield, with the intention of establishing a home for disabled servicemen. Owing to a severe lack of hospital beds, it was converted into a hospital which mainly treated orthopaedic cases, with the Red Cross providing the equipment and some of the beds donated by various organisations. Once patients were sufficiently recovered from their injuries, outings were arranged for them with local motorists providing transport at their own expense.

1917 There were several temporary hospitals in the Manchester area which treated those wounded at the front. This one was situated on Grange Street in Rusholme and may have been for officers. The proximity of the Infirmary and the presence of large houses capable to being converted into temporary hospitals made the Rusholme area very suitable for this type of hospital. Although the men were recovering from their wounds, it appears that Christmas was not forgotten, with decorations and a tree adding some festive cheer to the ward.

c. **1917** During the First World War, flying came of age with aircraft being used for reconnaissance purposes as well as trying to shoot down barrage balloons and attack enemy aircraft positions. Over 4,000 Avro 504s were constructed by the firm in Manchester, out of a total wartime production of 8,300. Whether this is an Avro 504 is not certain, but it is clear that it has attracted a lot of attention in Albert Square, where it has been put on display. As well as manufacturing aircraft there was a small airfield on Princess Road, Withington, where completed aircraft were brought together before being sent out to the front line.

1919 Another innovation in the First World War was the use of tanks. This one was photographed as it passed through central Manchester with an armed foot escort. The presence of the tank appears to have attracted a large crowd of onlookers, who would have read about them in the newspapers and might have seen them on film at the cinema. Not only would the tanks have been very noisy, but the clouds of exhaust at the rear would have created quite a smell. This tank went on display in Platt Fields, possibly as a thank-you to Mancunians for their efforts during the war.

1916 As the threat from submarines increased during the war, so food shortages started to arise and rationing had to be introduced. This queue of housewives is outside Jackson's Market in Moss Side, presumably after a delivery of fresh vegetables.

1917 The original caption of this photograph is 'Communal Kitchen', although it looks like a place where hot meals were provided. Whether the aim of the organisers was to give children a hot meal when their mothers were at work in the local factories or whether fuel shortages made it difficult to provide regular hot meals is not clear. It does, however, indicate that there was hardship at home as well as at the front.

1918 Manchester docks played an important role in the war effort as the shipping was safe from enemy raids while it was being unloaded. Raw materials, armaments and foodstuffs were all imported through the docks and distributed throughout the region by rail. Towards the end of the war, the docks saw the arrival of American troops on their way to the front. These Americans were disembarking from the *City of Exeter* after their journey across the Atlantic.

1929 The First World War ended on 11 November 1918, its effect on those who fought and the families of those who were killed or injured was long-lasting. Between and after the wars, 11 November each year became a time for people to remember those who had given their lives. It was originally intended to erect Manchester's war memorial in Albert Square, but it was not possible to reorder the statues quickly enough so it was set up in St Peter's Square as a temporary measure. Here the Cenotaph is guarded by troops with reversed rifles while members of the British Limbless Ex-Servicemen's Association (BLESMA) march past, watched by a huge crowd.

1933 Although the Cenotaph was in St Peter's Square, the two minutes' silence and following service were observed by large crowds, led by the Lord Mayor, in Albert Square as it was the only place large enough to accommodate such a gathering. This is the scene in 1933 as a huge crowd stands silently observing the two minutes' silence. After the service, the Lord Mayor led the tributes by laying a wreath at the Cenotaph, followed by representatives of a large number of Manchester's organisations.

Between the Wars

1937   After the controversy surrounding the abdication of Edward VIII, the coronation of George VI was greeted with a sigh of relief by Mancunians. The centre of Manchester was decorated with banners hung from lampposts, like these on King Street. A full programme of civic events was organised which included open-air services in Heaton Park, Platt Fields and Wythenshawe Park, and band concerts in many of the other city parks. As electric lighting was far more widespread than it had been in 1910, many buildings were floodlit for the occasion. At night, illuminated tram cars and buses toured the city's streets.

1924 This spectacular display of posters, close to the junction of London Road and Piccadilly, would have been clearly visible to those using London Road as well as to those using the approach to London Road station. It appears that the posters have been stuck directly on to the brickwork of the building so that only the doors and windows are left uncovered. The picture gives a good indication of what people were being persuaded to spend their money on at that time, ranging from consumer products to places of entertainment. It is interesting to note that E.R. Buck & Sons Ltd, who manufactured sports wear with the brand name 'Bukta' and who occupied the former Piccadilly cotton mill, have taken the opportunity to advertise their own products on the upper part of the wall. The former mill has now been demolished, but the small building on the left of the photograph, known as the Coach and Horses and dating from the late eighteenth century when it was an artisan's home and workshop, still survives, although in a derelict state. To the right of the mill is the Joshua Hoyles building, erected in 1904, which has recently been converted into a hotel.

1936   On the day of George V's funeral on 28 January 1936, a memorial service was held at Manchester Cathedral, attended by leaders of local government, and representatives of local industry and of the many organisations involved in the life of the city. Those attending gathered at the Town Hall and processed to the cathedral, led by the band of the 2nd Battalion of the Manchester Regiment. This is the scene inside the cathedral as the Bishop of Manchester preaches his sermon.

1937   When George VI was crowned in May, the Lord Mayor of Manchester expressed the hope that everyone would enjoy themselves and that celebrations would be held in all parts of the city. Apart from the official celebrations, which included a civic service and the broadcasting of the coronation service in Albert Square, many street parties like this one in Gorton were held, organised by the residents. As a memento of the occasion, ex-servicemen, pensioners and children received gifts of either a decorated box of chocolates, a fountain pen or a book.

1929 In 1912, Manchester Free Reference Library was forced to leave its premises in the former Town Hall at the corner of Cross Street and King Street, as the building had been declared unsafe. As a temporary measure, the Reference Library was housed in temporary buildings on part of the site of the former Infirmary in Piccadilly. Plans to erect a new library had to be postponed when war broke out in 1914 so the stay in Piccadilly became protracted. Although approval to build the new library was granted in 1920, the new building was not completed and opened until 1934.

1930 The new Central Library was designed by Vincent Harris, who chose a circular shape with a large, domed central reading room and offices and other facilities in the outside curtain wall. The foundation stone of the new library was laid by the Prime Minister, Ramsay Macdonald, on 6 May 1930 in front of a large crowd. This photograph of the laying of the foundation stone also shows the tops of the some of the buildings on the adjacent site, between the Town Hall and the library, which were soon to be demolished to enable the Town Hall Extension to be built.

1934 In this year George V and Queen Mary visited Manchester for the third time. The reason for the visit was to receive on behalf of the Manchester Regiment, of which he was Colonel-in-Chief, four silver drums given to it by Manchester. During the same visit, the king laid the foundation stone of the Town Hall Extension, designed by Vincent Harris, and officially opened the new Central Library, which had cost £413,000 and was capable of holding a million books. The removal of the Reference Library from Piccadilly early in 1934 took place without the loss of a single day's opening. Here the king and queen leave the library after performing the opening and making their way to their car, which took them to Liverpool, on the way to which they also opened the newly completed East Lancashire Road.

1936 When Manchester acquired Piccadilly from the Infirmary and demolished the old hospital in 1910, there was much discussion of an appropriate use for the site. Various suggestions were made for commercial development of part of it, including a new exchange. However, no decision was taken and the site was landscaped apart from a small corner where an outpatients' department was built by the Infirmary and later huts erected for the Reference Library. By 1936 the library huts and the outpatients' department had been cleared and the whole site was a public open space.

1938 One part of central Manchester where there was considerable change in the late 1920s and 1930s was between Lloyd Street, Cooper Street, St Peter's Square, Peter Street and Mount Street, which were cleared for the new central library and the Town Hall Extension. Other work affected the site formerly occupied by St Peter's Church when the Cenotaph was placed at one end and its landscaping improved. The result was that by 1939, St Peter's Square was far more attractive than it had been 20 years earlier, although traffic remained a serious problem as the church site was treated as a large roundabout.

c. **1935** The Hippodrome on Oxford Street opened at the end of 1904 as a variety theatre with facilities to stage spectacular shows. However, with the growth of cinemas and the arrival of the 'talkies' in the late 1920s, interest in variety theatres declined. In 1935 its owners, Bernstein Cinemas, decided to convert it into a 2,500-seat luxury cinema, which involved demolishing a substantial part of the building, to be known as the Granada. Shortly before it opened, however, it was purchased by Gaumont British and renamed the Gaumont. The new cinema was opened by Jessie Matthews and her husband, Sonny Hale, and was regarded as the most luxurious cinema in Manchester.

1923   On 15 November 1922 those Mancunians with wireless sets were able to pick up the following message: '2ZY calling, 2ZY calling. Our transmission tonight will consist of late news followed by musical items. At 7 p.m. we shall send a short story to children followed by music, after which election results will be transmitted up to 11 p.m.' Thus began the first broadcast by the BBC from a temporary studio at the Metropolitan Vickers works in Trafford Park. The studio remained there for less than 12 months before moving first to 57 Dickenson Street, then to Orme Buildings in St Mary's Parsonage and finally to Piccadilly in 1928. This photograph of the original studio shows the heavy cloth hung around the walls to improve the acoustics, the announcer's desk and lights wjich linked the studio with the engineers outside as well as the station's grand piano, pianola, gramophone and microphone,

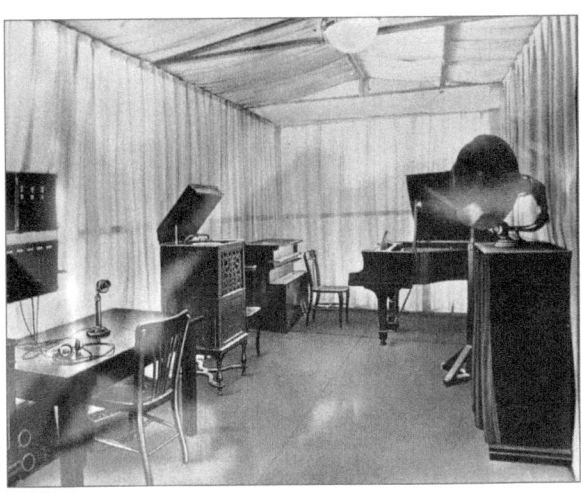

1927   Although the motor car was making advances, cycling still retained much of its pre-war appeal, especially where racing was concerned. Here is shown the start of a 10-mile race for the National Cycling Union (Manchester centre) championship. Where the race was held and whether the contestants were drawn from the dock police is not clear, but it is possible that the venue was the Manchester Athletic Club's grounds in Fallowfield, which had a banked cycle track.

1920   On 27 March 1920, King George V attended the First Division match between Manchester City and Liverpool at Manchester's Hyde Road ground. This was the first time that the king had attended a professional football match outside London. He is seen being introduced to the Manchester City team which included the legendary Max Woosnam, who not only played football, but was an all-rounder winning blues in athletics, cricket, golf, rackets, tennis and football. He also won a tennis gold medal at the Antwerp Olympics of 1920 and the men's doubles championship at Wimbledon the following year. He joined Manchester City in 1920; the team then went 18 months without a home defeat.

c. **1935** One of the most popular places
of entertainment in Manchester during
the first half of the century was Belle Vue,
which combined a zoo with an amusement
park. Belle Vue had been established by
John Jennison in 1836 and had gradually
expanded, with new animals and activities
being added each year. In 1925, the Jennison
family relinquished their control over
developments at Belle Vue and although
facilities for the animals were improved,
much more was spent on improving the
amusement park. However, some of the old
attractions remained such as the open air
dance floor shown here in the 1930s and the
firework displays with their spectacular sets.

1920s During the 1920s and '30s, a programme of slum clearance was introduced, with the intention of getting rid of some of the very poorest housing in the inner city area. Progress was slow because the government controlled the amount of money that the council could spend, and because land on which to build the new council estates had to be acquired. The type of property which Manchester sought to deal with was similar to that shown here – apparently back-to-back houses, if the washing hanging across the street is any guide.

1937 Manchester is regarded as an industrial city, but when it absorbed Wythenshawe in 1931, it acquired a large rural area in north Cheshire. The intention of the City Council was to develop the area for housing so that residents from the slums could be rehoused in what Lloyd George had described in 1919 as 'homes fit for heroes'. It was some time before the first houses were built and not until after the Second World War that building and the provision of supporting facilities could start in earnest. This view shows Woodhouse Lane in 1937 with the typical style of council house that was erected between the wars.

1939 A major enlargement of the Royal Exchange planned before the First World War had to be postponed when war broke out. When the work was eventually completed and the enlarged building opened by George V in 1921, the cotton industry had begun to decline. Membership of the Exchange began to fall which meant that the company had to find other sources of income to meet the cost of maintaining the building. During the 1930s, the main floor of the Royal Exchange was hired as a ballroom while the offices surrounding the floors were let to both members and non-members. Although the cotton industry was in decline, Manchester still remained the financial and commercial centre of the industry, as this photograph of the floor of the Exchange shows.

1934 When William and Colin Mather and W.W. Platt took over Bateman & Sherratt's Salford Iron Works in the 1830s, Manchester was developing into an important engineering centre making steam engines, self-acting mules and machine tools. This development continued throughout the nineteenth century with companies beginning to diversify into new fields of engineering. In 1882, William Mather visited America where he met Thomas Edison, which resulted in the firm beginning to manufacture dynamos. Between 1900 and 1912, the company gradually moved its operations to a 45-acre site in Newton Heath. This is Mather & Platt's machine shop in 1934 when the company was making a wide range of products from fire extinguishers to textile machinery.

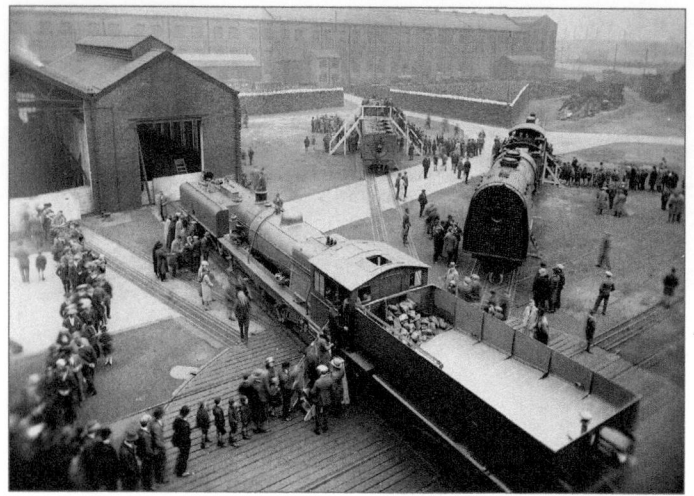

1928 One of the city's best-known firms was Beyer Peacock & Co. of Gorton, which manufactured railway engines, many of which were sent abroad. Like other firms at this time the company went through a difficult period, but survived and made an important contribution to the war effort and post-war reconstruction of railways in other countries. Possibly the company's most famous type of locomotive was the Beyer-Garratt, which worked extensively in Africa. The Beyer-Garratt locomotive seen here had been built either for the Nitrate Railways or the Kenya–Uganda Railway and was on display at an open day organised to raise money for the Manchester Medical Charities Fund, which raised £278.

1934 Although older forms of engineering continued in and around Manchester, new forms also made their appearance. One of the most important was the construction of aeroplanes by Avro in Newton Heath. This company had gradually expanded in the 1920s and by 1934 took over another 250,000 square ft of floor space to produce Avians and Cadets for flying clubs and Tudors for the RAF, all of which were single-engined planes. This photograph shows the framework of a new aircraft, possibly an Avian, under assembly.

1934 Although heavy industry remained a major employer of labour in Manchester between the wars, new industries did make their appearance. One was the electronics industry as typified by Ferranti's. Initially, the firm made domestic appliances such as electric irons and electric fires, but gradually diversified into making parts for radios and later televisions. Here, the workers are assembling radio valves at the recently completed factory in Moston where conditions were much pleasanter than in the older industrial concerns.

1926 Like other towns and cities, Manchester was affected by the General Strike which took place between 4 and 12 May 1926. As public transport ground to a halt with few trains and no trams running, getting to work could be a problem, although a limited service within a short distance of the centre of Manchester was provided by privately owned buses and taxis. Many firms, however, carried on with little disruption during the strike while their employees found novel ways of getting to work such as these bowler-hatted men on the back of a lorry. Some of them are enjoying it while others appear less than happy about travelling in such a vehicle.

1926 A view of Piccadilly during the General Strike as a few lorries carry essential supplies to the markets. Towards the end of the strike, three lorries were reported to have been attacked and destroyed by strikers, but on the whole the situation remained relatively calm throughout the period. Local newspapers were badly affected with the *Manchester Evening News* publishing only a duplicated broadsheet. Electricity supplies were not cut although the unions had threatened that if the council ran the trams, this would happen.

1931 Like other towns and cities Manchester experienced high levels of unemployment especially in the older, heavy industries such as engineering. This led to protest marches. One such occasion was on 3 October 1931 when 10,000 people took part in a march from All Saints to Quay Street, organised by the Manchester and Salford Trades Council. This passed off peacefully, but four days later, a march organised by the National Unemployment Workers Movement which was intended to go from Ardwick Green to Albert Square was broken up by the police and 26 were arrested as a result of clashes with the police.

1830–1930

THIS TABLET IS AFFIXED TO
THE FIRST MANCHESTER RAILWAY STATION
TO COMMEMORATE THE CENTENARY OF THE INAUGURATION OF THE
LIVERPOOL AND MANCHESTER RAILWAY ∷ IT WAS UNVEILED BY THE
LORD MAYORS OF LIVERPOOL AND MANCHESTER ON SEPT. 15TH 1930.

LAWRENCE DURNING HOLT,
LORD MAYOR OF LIVERPOOL.

ROBERT NOTON BARCLAY,
LORD MAYOR OF MANCHESTER.

1930 In 1930, the centenary of the opening of the world's first inter-city passenger railway, using steam engines to haul passengers, was celebrated in Manchester by the unveiling of this plaque on front of Liverpool Road station, the original Manchester terminus of the line. Liverpool Road only operated as a passenger station between 1830 and 1844, after which it became a goods depot and remained in use as such until the mid-1970s, when it was closed. Through the efforts of the Liverpool Road Station Society and the former Greater Manchester Council, the original station building, the original warehouse and two of the remaining three later warehouses were converted into the Museum of Science and Industry in Manchester.

1931 During the 1920s and '30s, the railway companies were forced to look at ways of improving their services in order to compete with the electric trams and growing numbers of motor buses and motor cars. In 1916, the line between Manchester and Bury had been successfully electrified and by the late 1920s, plans were prepared to electrify the busy commuter line between Manchester and Altrincham. The work, completed in 1931 at a cost of £500,000, not only speeded up the journey, but also enabled more trains to be run. The new trains and the journey were described as being 'big, comfortable and roomy, with a steadiness and smoothness that makes the journey a pleasant break between the office and home'. The new trains were introduced on 11 May 1931 and soon found favour with commuters.

1929 Although there had been a few commercial flights from an airfield close to the junction of Princess Road and Mauldeth Road West in the years immediately after the First World War, it was not until 1928 that there was any serious interest in establishing an aerodrome to serve Manchester. A letter to the *Manchester Guardian* from a John Leeming advocating such a move appears to have aroused the interest of the Council which in turn led to Manchester becoming determined to have the first municipal aerodrome in the country. The licence was granted on 19 April 1929 with effect from 22 April. This photograph shows the Lord Mayor, Alderman George Westcott, and the delegation which had flown to London to collect the all-important licence, arriving back at Manchester.

1930s The site Manchester chose for its new airport was at Barton, although until the site was ready aircraft operated from a temporary airstrip at Rackhouse. However, it soon became obvious that Barton was not ideal and, following a very critical report from Captain Smirnoff, KLM's chief pilot, it was decided to find an alternative site. This site was at Ringway, on the edge of Wythenshawe, which had just been incorporated into Manchester. This 1930s photograph shows Barton aerodrome with a crowd of spectators on the ground, possibly at an air show.

1932 When the Manchester Ship Canal was opened in 1894, it provided the city with a direct link to the sea. After a slow start, the amount of traffic using the canal gradually increased. It was reported that in the year 1921–2, almost 1 million tons of shipping passed along the waterway. The volume of goods carried also rose steadily, passing the 6 million ton mark in 1926 and 7 million a decade later. The Ship Canal was always busy with ships from all parts of the world. This particular ship is the SS *Mahronda* of the Brocklehurst Lines, making its way to Manchester possibly from ports east of Suez.

1938 The Manchester and Salford Junction Canal was opened in 1838 to link the Rochdale Canal with the River Irwell. In 1872 the canal was purchased by the Cheshire Lines Committee, as part of its route crossed where the railway wanted to build Central station. As a result, the section between the Rochdale Canal and Watson Street was closed. The section from Watson Street to the river continued to be used until 1922 to get goods to the Great Northern Warehouse, but then this too was abandoned. This photograph, taken in 1938, shows the entrance to the tunnel section of the canal at Water Street, which has now been blocked off. Behind the photographer is the lock which enabled vessels to enter the river from the canal, which can still seen today from the grounds of the Victoria and Albert Hotel.

1920s During the period between the two world wars, the number of cars and motor lorries on the roads of Manchester increased dramatically and began to cause traffic congestion, which was tackled by means of one-way systems and the arrival of parking restrictions. The amount of horse-drawn traffic declined sharply as the internal combustion engine took hold. Portland Street in the 1920s accommodated not only motor cars and motor lorries, but also horse-drawn vehicles and a steam wagon while in the background is an electric tram.

1932 As the number of motor cars, lorries and even motor buses increased so the crossing of roads became that much more dangerous, especially for children and elderly people. Outside the Eye Hospital on Oxford Road, what was described as a 'safety zone' was created. This appears to have been pedestrian-operated traffic lights so that pedestrians could cross the road in safety. It is possible that the photograph records the first day, with a policeman in attendance to help both motorists and pedestrians get accustomed to the new system.

1933 Although trams remained the most important form of public road transport between the wars, there was a gradual move towards introducing buses, which some regarded as more flexible. They did not involve the heavy capital expenditure for overhead wires and the laying of tracks. In 1937, Manchester took the decision to convert all its tram routes to bus operation as soon as it was practical to do so. Here trams and buses stand alongside each other on Portland Street waiting for the policeman to stop the traffic on Oxford Street.

1926 In 1926, Manchester staged what was known as Civic Week during which the Council put on displays for its citizens of its achievements in the past and its aspirations for the future. At about the same time Wythenshawe Hall, Park and Gardens, given by the Simons to Manchester, were opened to the public. To mark the occasion, a pageant was held which involved the re-enactment of the Siege of Wythenshawe Hall during 1643 and 1644. The cast of around 50 people was drawn from Northendon Amateur Dramatic Society, the Comrades Club and Music Society, and attracted a lot of interest among local people and Mancunians.

1938 In October 1838, Manchester was granted borough status, which replaced the Court Leet and Police Commissioners with a modern form of local government. In 1853, two years after Queen Victoria's visit to Manchester, it received city status. The right to call its first citizen 'Lord Mayor' dates from 1893. In 1938, the city celebrated its centenary with a week-long exhibition at the City Hall on Liverpool Road, which showed various facets of the work of the council. In addition, there was a civic banquet and service together with a visit by George VI, who opened the Town Hall Extension. The banquet shown here took place in the Midland Hotel on 25 April 1938. It was organised by Allied Newspapers as its contribution to mark the centenary of Manchester's incorporation. The guests included leaders from all aspects of life in Manchester as well as distinguished Mancunians. Among the speakers were David Lloyd George and Lord Kelmsley.

The Second World War

1940 One of the buildings that was damaged in the Christmas blitz
was the Royal Exchange, where part of the trading floor and roof were
affected. The damage forced members of the Exchange to move to the
Houldsworth Hall, but after a brief period, as the temporary premises
were not satisfactory, repairs were made to the Royal Exchange building
and members returned to their traditional home. Here smoke is seen
pouring out of the tower of the building as a hose, which appears to be
lashed to the top of the ladder, plays water on the fire.

1938 As the storm clouds darkened over Europe in the late 1930s Britain began to rearm and prepare for war. This group of women from the Women's Legion Mechanical Transport Section, founded during the First World War, are receiving training in how to maintain an internal combustion engine. They were also trained in ambulance work and anti-gas measures. All the volunteers were expected to be competent drivers and aged between eighteen and forty.

1939 In order to protect the population from air attack, it was decided that there should be a programme of providing air raid shelters. In the centre of Manchester and in the densely populated inner city areas there were public shelters, but in those areas where people had gardens Anderson shelters were provided. These were made of corrugated iron and were meant to be partially buried, the recommended depth being up to 4 ft in the ground and the roof covered with 15 inches of soil. Here a family sets about discovering how to erect the shelter while the family dog watches with interest.

1939 The authorities were not only worried about conventional high explosive and incendiary bombs, but they also feared that the Germans might use gas to attack the civilian population. Everyone, including babies, was equipped with gas masks which were to be carried at all times. Belle Vue even insisted that you showed your gas mask when you entered the amusement park while the Education Department pointed out that 99 per cent of all elementary schoolchildren carried theirs with them all the time. This photograph shows ARP wardens delivering a baby's gas mask to a young mother somewhere in Manchester.

1939 In April 1939, Manchester drew up plans to evacuate all children to the country. The city was allocated almost 180,000 places in surrounding counties where it was thought there was less risk of raids. The decision to implement the evacuation was taken in the middle of August with the first evacuees to leave on 1 September and the whole operation to be completed by 3 September. This was achieved with the co-operation of the transport authorities, the police and the organisational ability of the teachers involved. The children either walked or were taken by bus or tram to a railway station, each group of 10 being accompanied by an adult. Children here are about to board a tram to the station, each carrying a rucksack or bag containing only a change of clothing and their gas mask while anxious parents look on.

1940 Manchester was raided by the German air force on two consecutive nights, 22/3 and 23/4 December, the so-called Christmas blitz. A large part of central Manchester was severely damaged, including the warehouses behind Piccadilly, shown above. The Christmas blitz affected some 31 acres within a one-mile radius of the Town Hall. It destroyed 200 business premises, 165 warehouses, 150 offices and 5 banks, and severely damaged over 1,000 other buildings.

1940 This is the view of the area between Piccadilly and York Street from the top of Lewis's store a few days after the Christmas blitz when some of the rubble had been moved and the fires extinguished. The destruction had been made worse by a rising wind which had blown burning embers into less severely damaged buildings, starting more fires. By the end of the second night's raid, the Fire Service calculated that there were 6 conflagrations, 20 major fires and over 600 other outbreaks which had to be dealt with.

1940 The heroes of the Manchester Christmas blitz were undoubtedly the men of the fire service who courageouly fought to contain the fires and prevent them spreading to important buildings like the Central Telephone Exchange and the Dickenson Street power station. They were hampered in their work by the fact that the main water supply into the city was cut so they had to rely on supplies obtained from canals and rivers. At the height of the blitz, over 400 additional fire appliances and 3,400 men were brought in from the surrounding area. These men are fighting a blaze in a building on Portland Street while behind them is the burned-out shell of a warehouse.

1940 One of the buildings that was destroyed in the Christmas raids was the Free Trade Hall, described by the Lord Mayor on the following morning as 'a symbol of Manchester's greatness'. All that remained of Edward Walter's splendid building were the outer walls. The interior, which had seen so many memorable events since the building opened in 1856, was left a tangled ruin, with the columns and girders which formerly supported the balcony and gallery all that can be identified as part of the interior of the building.

1940 As well as severely damaging the Piccadilly area, the two nights' bombing also caused considerable damage around the Market Place. This photograph was taken from Cateaton Street, looking along Old Millgate towards the Market Place and the Royal Exchange. Although the devastation was extensive, one building, the Wellington Inn, escaped virtually unscathed from the bombing while in the background, the tower of the Royal Exchange looms out of the murk. Among the buildings destroyed in this area were the Coal Exchange, the Bull's Head Hotel, the Falstaff Hotel and Victoria Buildings.

1940 Although it did not receive a direct hit, the Lady Chapel, the Ely Chapel and part of the Derby or Regimental Chapel at Manchester Cathedral were destroyed by a parachute mine landing close by. Within 24 hours of the damage occurring, discussions were under way with the cathedral's architect, Hubert Worthington, and a Wilmslow timber expert, James Brown, about the best way to protect the medieval woodwork which had escaped serious damage and about the cathedral's restoration.

1940 Two of central Manchester's transport facilities that were particularly badly damaged in the December blitz were Exchange and Victoria stations. The main office block at the front of Exchange station was destroyed while a land mine severely damaged platforms 14 to 17 at Victoria station. In addition to the damage done to the railways, overhead tram wires were also brought down, making it difficult for tram services to be quickly restored.

1940 Although there was much damage to public and commercial buildings as well as to Manchester's infrastructure, there was also serious damage done to Manchester's housing stock. Throughout the war, 389 houses were destroyed and a further 1,562 so badly damaged that they had to be demolished. These houses once stood on Caton Street in Hulme, but all that was left after the raid were the back and part walls, the fronts having being blown off by the blast.

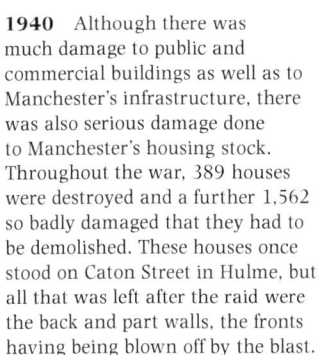

1941 Although not as severe as the Christmas blitz, Manchester suffered a second major raid on 1 June 1941. It lasted 90 minutes, and caused further serious damage to several factories and public buildings. Among those which were affected by the Whitsun raid were the Assize Courts at Strangeways, shown here together with the Woolpack Inn, which was a favourite with the legal profession attending the courts, several factories and the Jewish Hospital in Crumpsall.

1941 After the Christmas blitz, a large area behind Piccadilly lay devastated and eventually the burnt-out buildings were demolished. This photograph is dated 20 August 1941, some eight months after the raid, and shows the view from Portland Street, looking towards Mosley Street, after demolition. In the background are the towers of the Town Hall and the Midland Bank on King Street; the block in the centre shows the ruins of the home of the Manchester Literary and Philosophical Society on George Street. Once the area had been cleared of rubble, some of the basements of destroyed buildings were turned into static water tanks to provide additional supplies of water should there be another major air raid.

1941 Early in 1941, George VI and Queen Elizabeth visited Manchester and toured the ruined streets. Here the king is seen passing some of the devastation in Piccadilly. As well as Piccadilly, the royal party visited the Royal Exchange and inspected men from the fire service in the playground at Chetham's School.

1941 Another visitor to Manchester to inspect the damage caused by the blitz was Winston Churchill, seen here in the ruins of the Free Trade Hall, where in January 1940 he was reported to have called on his audience to 'Let us to the task, to the battle, to the toil'. Although his visit in April 1941 was meant to have been 'secret', news of it soon spread and he was welcomed by large cheering crowds.

c. **1942** There was a programme of collecting metal, paper, textiles and anything else that could be used in the war effort. During the first year Manchester's salvage effort realised 8,151 tons of metal, worth £23,250, and 4,029 tons of paper, worth £17,060. These amounts did not include material salvaged from the few buildings that were hit by stray bombers early in 1940. After the Christmas blitz, there was a considerable amount of material, especially metal and stone, which was salvaged for possible re-use. Although most of the centres for the collection of salvage were at cleansing depots, occasionally parks, like Heaton Park, were used.

1942 Throughout the war, members of the public were encouraged to invest in National Savings. From time to time there were special campaigns to raise money for a specific purpose. Between 21 and 28 February 1942, Manchester staged 'Warship Week' with the aim of raising £10 million. In Lewis's there was a Royal Navy exhibition, while in Pauldens the RAF put on a display. In Piccadilly there were daily displays of unarmed combat and fire fighting. The centre-piece was a large model of HMS *Nelson* in Piccadilly, which also doubled as a saluting platform. The whole event raised £12½ million or £2 13s 4d for every man, woman and child in Manchester.

1945 To mark the end of almost 6 years of war in Europe 8 May 1945 was designated as VE Day. All but essential services were closed down for two days while people celebrated in the streets. The official ceremonies started with a service in the cathedral followed by an official announcement of the end of hostilities in Europe from the steps of the Town Hall and the unfurling of the flags of the 44 founder members of the United Nations.

1945 The complete cessation of all hostilities came with the surrender of the Japanese on 14/15 August. Although it was midnight when the news came through, central Manchester was soon filled with dancing and singing crowds. The news was officially announced by the Lord Mayor at 10 a.m. and this was followed by a civic service of thanksgiving in the cathedral. Throughout Manchester, bands played in parks, services were held in churches and impromptu street parties organised. In the evening, illuminated trams and buses toured the city while at 9 p.m. George VI's message to the nation was relayed by loudspeaker in Albert Square.

The Postwar Period

c. 1959 Many people who are associated with Manchester were not born and bred in the city, but came here either to study or to take up a position with some company or organisation. One such person whose name became synonymous with music, especially the Hallé Orchestra, in the years after 1943, was Sir John Barbirolli. He was invited to Manchester to reconstruct the Hallé Orchestra and stayed with it for the rest of his life. Between 1943 and 1958, he was the orchestra's permanent conductor, becoming its Conductor-in-Chief in 1958 and Conductor Laureate to the Hallé in 1968. Barbirolli died in 1970, having become a legend in Manchester during his lifetime.

1945 As soon as the war in Europe had ended, Churchill called a general election. He opened his campaign in Manchester with a short speech before a crowd estimated to be around 80,000. However, in spite of his popularity as a prime minister, the country rejected the Conservatives and Labour won a landslide victory. In Manchester, five of the seven seats went to Labour, leaving the Conservatives with only Withington and Bucklow, which included Wythenshawe.

1945 This photograph may have been taken in the churchyard of the former All Saints Church in Chorlton-on-Medlock and shows delegates to the fifth Pan-African Congress, which was held in Chorlton Town Hall. Among those present were several future leaders of African states, including Jomo Kenyatta and Kwame Nkrumah.

1945   In his speech to the assembled crowd in front of the Town Hall on 15 August 1945, the Lord Mayor looked forward to a new future, a future which would involve much reconstruction and replacement of buildings damaged as a result of the blitz. A similar sentiment about the future and people's aspirations for it was expressed in this tableau, entitled 'The Future is Ours', which formed part of a May Day celebration held in June 1945, organised by the Manchester and Salford Council for Labour.

1946   The Co-operative Movement was very strong in and around Manchester with many districts having their own independent co-operative societies. These societies formed important parts of the local community with their members taking part in local events. This float was prepared by the Blackley Co-operative Society in 1946, but it is not certain whether it was for a local event or a co-operative rally. The theme of the float, however, is very clear – education and its importance to all.

1948 With the return to peace in 1945 and the election of a Labour Government in the same year, some sections of society expected things to change far more quickly than was possible. This demonstration had been organised by the Manchester branch of the Communist Party outside Manchester Town Hall. The protesters appear to be complaining about the speed at which new homes were being provided. It was a protest more against the government than against Manchester as a local authority and its activities.

1953 When the war ended in 1945, there was the expectation that rationing would cease, but this was not the case. According to some reports, the amounts of food people were entitled to barely increased during the late 1940s and bread was rationed for the first time. However, in the early 1950s, rationing was gradually removed. This queue of adults and children are outside a shop in Wythenshawe the day sweets were taken off ration. No wonder they look so cheerful as, for the first time in almost 15 years, they could buy whatever they wanted, provided they could afford it and there were supplies available.

1950s Although Manchester had drawn up plans to remove the remaining slums in the city, it was a policy which took time to implement and required not only money to build new houses, but also land where the houses could be built. It was not only the remaining courts like this one, Span Court, that were to be cleared, but whole areas of terraced housing which were regarded as not capable of being improved to a satisfactory standard.

1950s One area where many new council houses were built was Wythenshawe, which for many years resembled a giant construction site. Several different types of houses were built there to cater for the different needs of the tenants. Some wanted family houses while others only wanted flats. The problem with Wythenshawe was that although people lived there, there was little employment and so the residents had to travel back into Manchester to work, which increased their cost of living.

1949 On 10 January 1949, the last tram operated by Manchester Corporation Tramways Department was driven from Piccadilly to the Birchfields Road depot by the committee's chairman, Councillor Barratt, watched by a large crowd. Its journey marked the end of a system of public transport which had served Mancunians well for almost 48 years, but was not as flexible as the buses which replaced it for the changing traffic conditions of the postwar period.

1959 Although trams disappeared from Manchester's streets in 1949, trolley buses continued to be used on several routes to the east of Manchester. Trolley buses were regarded as more flexible than trams as they could move to the kerb when stopping and did not obstruct traffic. This view shows Piccadilly looking towards London Road station which was used by a large number of buses and trolley buses heading for Fairfield Street, Hyde Road and Stockport Road. At this time, the cars are outnumbered by the buses and trolley buses leaving central Manchester.

1954 When war broke out in 1939, work on electrifying the railway line through the Woodhead tunnel between Manchester and Sheffield was suspended. After the war, the plans were revived and work restarted. This involved boring a second tunnel through the Pennines at Woodhead. The modernised line was opened in 1954 providing a cleaner and faster journey between the two cities as well as giving the towns and communities between Manchester and Glossop an electrified commuter service. This view shows two of the locomotives built for the line outside London Road station.

1948 In 1946, Ringway Airport was handed back to Manchester after being requisitioned and used during the war by the military. In June 1946, the first passenger services were introduced with an Air France service between Manchester and Paris. Gradually, the number of services increased and as passenger levels improved, so it became necessary to expand the terminal buildings. By the end of the 1950s, Manchester was not only linked to Europe by air, but also to North America with regular transatlantic flights. This photograph shows the terminal buildings in 1948, before the expansion programme was started.

1947 Manchester had always maintained a strict attitude towards places of entertainment opening on Sundays. After a long discussion, it was agreed that Manchester's cinemas could open on Sundays for the duration of the war. At the end of the war, cinemas continued to open on Sundays, but in 1947 the question was raised again with a powerful lobby demanding the return to the pre-war position. A town meeting held in April agreed that the matter should be decided by a ballot, which was held on 8 May. In the poll, 17,140 were in favour of Sunday cinemas and 7,676 against. As a result, cinemas in Manchester were allowed to continue opening on Sundays.

1949 This is part of the immense queue which built up hoping to get tickets to see Danny Kaye at the Palace Theatre between 13 and 18 June. It was stated that 25,000 tried to get tickets for a show which was said to have the audience rolling in the aisles with laughter.

c. **1950** Although there were several theatres and places of entertainment on Oxford Street, there were also a number on Peter Street, including the former Gaiety Theatre. Built in 1870 as the Comedy Theatre, the Gaiety achieved fame in the years before the First World War as the home of repertory theatre, championed by Annie Horniman. Between 1908 and about 1916, the Gaiety staged a number of important first performances including *Hindle Wakes.* In 1921, the theatre was converted into a cinema and remained in use as such until about 1959 when it was closed and demolished.

c. **1955** A quiet day on Cross Street (left) as a no. 41 bus picks up passengers outside the Royal Exchange. Although Longridge House on Corporation Street has been completed, work is only just beginning on Marks & Spencer's store at the corner of Market Street and Corporation Street. The right-hand picture shows the complete building a few years later as the Manchester City Police Band make a right turn from Market Street/St Mary's Gate into Cross Street at the head of a procession.

1950 A popular place for people to sit on a warm summer's day was Piccadilly Gardens, seen after the public air raid shelters had been removed. The work of the Parks Department with its floral clock attracts admiring glances from some while members of an older generation sit and and pass the time of day. Many of the buildings here date from the turn of the century although the Queen's Hotel (right) dates from the first half of the nineteenth century and the small building with 'LMS' over it is one of the original buildings erected when Piccadilly was known as Lever's Row at the beginning of the nineteenth century. This building is still standing today and is a visible link with the past of the area.

c. **1955** A typical Saturday afternoon scene on Cross Street as traffic congestion builds up. People would have come into central Manchester to visit some of the larger shops there. Although many people still came in by bus and train, an increasing number began to use their own cars, parking them at the side of the road and thus adding to the traffic problems.

1946 In February 1946, heavy rain caused serious problems in and around Manchester with the city's three main rivers bursting their banks. One area where there was very serious flooding was along the River Mersey, where hundreds of acres were inundated and Barnes Convalescent Home was cut off. It was said that the floods had been the worst for over 15 years. This photograph shows a horse being led to safety from a flooded field near Northendon.

1959 As there had been extensive damage done to the buildings around Piccadilly and the plans for rebuilding the area between Parker Street and York Street involved the closure of several streets which led directly into Piccadilly, the opportunity was taken to improve the road layout and the access to Parker Street bus station. The work that is going on here is the creation of a large island which would help pedestrians cross the road in safety. It is interesting to notice that there are far fewer bus stops on Piccadilly itself and that there is also two-way traffic along it.

1948 During the war, there had been great advances in electronics and a growing interest in developing ways of storing information electronically. In 1946, a team of experts gathered at Manchester University, including Tom Kilburn and F.C. Williams, to work on the problems associated with information storage, and produced a machine to do this. In June 1948, the team successfully tested their Mk 1 machine, which became, as far as can be ascertained, the world's first stored-programme computer. Compared with modern computers, this was a massive machine filling a whole room with equipment. It is also worth noting that parallel to the development of the computer, Dr A. Turing, also at Manchester University, worked on the development of computer programming.

1953 The work by Kilburn, Williams, Turing and others on the development of the computer ushered in a new era which had recently been described as the 'New Industrial Revolution'. The progress made in the last half century has been tremendous with computers getting ever smaller and at the same time more powerful. Four years after the first computer was developed, George VI died and was succeeded by his daughter Elizabeth II, thus beginning what some people called the 'New Elizabethan Age'. Her coronation in 1953 was the first where people could watch the ceremony live on television, but this did not stop the traditional street parties, bands in parks, firework displays and decorated buses touring the streets. It was as if with the accession of Elizabeth, the age of electronics dawned.

The 1960s and '70s

c. 1969 The 1960s saw an increase in the number of views of Manchester taken from aircraft or from the top floors of tall buildings. The result was some spectacular views of the city. Here the Mancunian Way is seen under construction at the end of the 1960s, snaking its way through Hulme and Chorlton-on-Medlock. Although the roundabout over the River Medlock where London Road and Downing Street meet has been completed and is in use, much of the elevated section has still be to constructed. Parts of Chorlton-on-Medlock and Hulme which have been cleared and will be redeveloped in the near future are also seen. Clearly identifiable are the Refuge Building, Gaythorn gas works, UMIST and the site of the former All Saints Church on Oxford Road.

***c.* 1970** The main feature of this aerial view is the large, partially cleared site bounded by Corporation Street, Market Street, High Street and Shudehill/ Withy Grove with Cannon Street running through the centre of the site, which is now covered by the Arndale Centre. The appearance of buildings which disappeared as the clearance work progressed is clearly seen. One building on Market Street, set back slightly from the remainder, was not demolished and is visible in the book's endpaper. Another interesting feature of the photograph is the fact that it shows buildings on Shudehill which were demolished when Metrolink was built and the front of the building now referred to as the Printworks on the corner of Withy Grove and Corporation Street. Other buildings which appear are the cathedral, the former Exchange station, Victoria station and buildings demolished as a result of the 1996 IRA bomb.

***c.* 1972** Looking westwards, Piccadilly Gardens and Piccadilly Plaza are seen while in the top right-hand corner there is the Town Hall, Town Hall Extension, Central Library and Midland Hotel. Also clearly visible is the Midland Bank on King Street, Ship Canal House, the warehouse of S. & J. Watts and the new premises for the Bank of England being constructed on Portland Street.

***c.* 1968** During the nineteenth and early twentieth centuries, Manchester suffered from a high level of smoke pollution which resulted in blackened buildings as well as causing health problems for residents. During the 1960s, a start was made cleaning public buildings, restoring damaged stonework and revealing architectural details which soot had hidden for many years. This is Waterhouse's Town Hall partially cleaned with the cleaned section contrasting with that section which still has to be dealt with.

***c.* 1965** This aerial photograph shows Manchester's earliest industrial suburb, Ancoats, development of which started in the late eighteenth century. Much has changed since this time, with many buildings having been demolished. However, Great Ancoats Street and the Rochdale Canal are still there, as are some of the mills on its banks. Also easily identifiable is the distinctive square of Victoria Buildings on Oldham Road and the tower of the former St Peter's Church on Blossom Street.

***c.* 1968** One of the earliest shopping arcades to be constructed in Manchester was the Lancaster Arcade which linked Fennel Street with Todd Street. This cast-iron, glass and wood structure was built in about 1853 and was the forerunner of arcades such as Barton Arcade. In its latter years, Lancaster Arcade was home to many small businesses, especially those specialising in numismatics and jewellery. Unfortunately, during the late 1960s, the building became neglected, businesses moved away and eventually, the arcade was demolished in the mid-1970s.

1970s Not photographed from an aircraft, but the top of a tall building in the university, this scene shows the skyline of central Manchester looking northwards. Among the buildings that can be identified are the Town Hall, Refuge Building, the chimney of Dickenson Street power station and Piccadilly Plaza. In the centre is the completed Mancunian Way, which from this height looks like a cordon around the southern part of the city centre. The vacant site where a building is shored up is now under development as the swimming pool for the Commonwealth Games of 2002.

c. **1965** In 1958, British Railways decided to electrify the main line from Manchester to London and to replace the booking hall and offices which had masked the train shed for almost a century. At the same time, the railway warehouses which lined one side of the approach to the station were demolished and replaced in the 1960s by Gateway House, which has been described as a lazy S in shape. At this time, most of the shop units at street level had not been taken.

1962 Pedestrians, cars and buses all vie for space at the junction of Princess Street and Portland Street. The 'limited stop' was one of a number of services operated by Manchester Corporation Transport Department which were designed to prevent buses serving the outer suburbs being filled with passengers who travelled only a few stops while those who lived further away had to wait for another bus, which might be 20 or 30 minutes later. The buildings in the background date from the first half of the nineteenth century when Portland Street terminated at this point.

***c.* 1970** When commercial television was established in 1956, Granada Television, which covered the north-west, established its studios and offices at the northern end of Manchester's entertainment area on Quay Street. Since that time the company has expanded, taking over part of the former Liverpool Road station goods depot for a theme park, Granada Studio Tours. This photograph, taken from the Hardman Street car park, shows Granada's studios as well as the Manchester College of Building and St John's College.

***c.* 1978** During the late 1950s and '60s, the number of pop groups increased dramatically, with performances taking place not only in theatres but also at dances in various city venues, often where students were to be found. Fly-posting became common with various bands and groups announcing where they were playing the following weekend. No empty building or hoarding was immune from the fly poster, as these on Hoyle's Building clearly show.

1963 An important date for Manchester University students was Shrove Tuesday, which was the occasion of the annual student rag when studies were forgotten in an effort to raise money for local charities. The main event was a procession of floats through the centre of Manchester, while student societies entertained passers-by with displays such as Morris dancing, here performing on the Esplanade in Piccadilly.

1978 The 1970s saw a revival of interest in Manchester's archaeological heritage. In 1972, the late Professor Barri Jones took the opportunity to excavate a site adjacent to the White Lion on Liverpool Road, where he found evidence of a Roman industrial site just outside the walls of the Roman fort that had once stood there. A few years later, as redevelopment was beginning to take place in the Tonman Street area, co-operation between the developers, the city council and university enabled several weeks excavation to be undertaken when more of the *vicus* or civilian settlement around the fort was discovered.

c. **1965** The Manchester City Police Band play as this procession of civic dignitaries and gentlemen wearing either top hats or bowler hats prepare to enter Manchester Cathedral for a service. It is not known what the event is, but it is possible that it is the annual Judges Sunday which took place at the beginning of the new legal year in October and was attended by the Lord Mayor and other members of the council and judiciary.

1960s During the 1960s, the Campaign for Nuclear Disarmament organised regular marches and protest meetings to draw attention to the threat posed by nuclear weapons. This demo is passing Sherratt & Hughes bookshop on Cross Street, going towards the Town Hall and Albert Square where a meeting would have been held.

c. **1972**   Cannon Street came into existence in the mid-eighteenth century. It is believed to have got its name because upturned cannons were used to prevent carts from breaking up the pavement as they turned corners. It was always a street of warehouses rather than shops, although, as can be seen, there were a few shops there in the 1960s and early '70s. At this time, the lower end of Cannon Street had already been demolished and work had started on constructing the Arndale Centre.

c. **1969**   This view along Market Street disappeared with the construction of the bridge linking the Arndale Centre with another new building on the corner of Cross Street and Market Street. On the left is Lewis's store while on the right is the site occupied by part of the Rylands empire for many years.

1960s A reminder of what Corporation Street and Cross Street looked like in the 1960s before the construction of the Arndale Centre. Compared with other streets in central Manchester, Corporation Street was relatively new, the first part having been completed in the late 1840s and the remainder to Miller Street in the 1850s. This new road provided a more direct route from the centre of Manchester to York Street, now Cheetham Hill Road.

c. **1965** The destruction of the area between Piccadilly and York Street during the war gave the opportunity for redevelopment to take place and provide Manchester with modern buildings. The new development, started in the 1960s, was not completed until the early 1970s and involved the construction of shops at street level with offices and a hotel on the upper levels. These are the two tower blocks, Sunley Building and Bernard House, under construction. Piccadilly Plaza, as the development was named, eventually came to dominate Piccadilly and the Gardens.

c. 1970   During the 1950s and 1960s, Tib Street was synonymous with pet shops as there were a number of them located there. The street itself follows the line of the River Tib, which disappeared from this area in the early nineteenth century. The Tib was little more than a stream when it was lost to view and one legend states that it was so narrow that on one occasion it was blocked by a cabbage stalk! The church in the background is St Paul's, New Cross, built in the 1870s and demolished in the 1980s.

1962   One of the main roads out of central Manchester to the south was Princess Street, which was lined on both sides with warehouses. This photograph shows homeward bound traffic in 1962 beginning to build up. Also in evidence are parking meters, which in 1999 are being replaced by pay and display on-street parking.

Modern Manchester

1999 When the Royal Exchange ceased to use the trading floor, there was a big question mark over the future of the building. Eventually, an imaginative solution was found to the problem, namely the construction of a theatre. This was designed to be theatre in the round without the need for elaborate stage sets and to allow members of the public and theatre-goers to appreciate the large former trading floor with its dome. The Royal Exchange Theatre opened with a production of *The Rivals* in September 1976. In June 1996, just a few months before the theatre was due to undergo major refurbishment, the building was damaged by the blast from an IRA bomb. Fortunately, it proved possible to restore the Royal Exchange building and undertake the refurbishment of the theatre, which was completed in 1998, continuing to provide Manchester with a magnificent theatre in the round set in a historic building.

***c*. 1980** Manchester's Lord Mayor's Show was introduced in the late 1970s and has now become a regular event in the summer, attracting visitors to the city centre as well as allowing firms and other organisations to publicise themselves in an attractive way. This is the float entered by one of Manchester's breweries, Wilson's, which had been established in 1842, as it passes across the junction of Princess Street and Portland Street.

1980 The 150th anniversary of the opening of the Liverpool and Manchester Railway was marked by a number of events including a cavalcade of railway locomotives at Rainhill and an exhibition at the former Liverpool Road station in Manchester, where a number of the locomotives which took part at Rainhill were displayed. To mark the occasion, the original station building was partially restored, as was a goods shed erected in the late 1850s, where many of the engines were exhibited. The original 1830 warehouse was cleaned although not restored for the event. Here, Royal Scot class locomotive 6115 Scots Guardsman stands next to a replica of one of the original passenger coaches from the Liverpool and Manchester Railway.

1992 When Castlefield Carnival was first introduced it ran for two days, but more recently it has been held only on the second Sunday of September. The event still attracts a large number of visitors although as it is only for a single day, few boats now attend compared with the early years of the event. The Staffordshire arm with its events arena is now the focal point of the carnival, although stalls and displays are to be found throughout the canal basin. This photograph shows the Staffordshire arms of the Bridgewater Canal at the 1992 carnival when the event was organised by the Castlefield Management Co. and the boating side by the Manchester branch of the Inland Waterways Association.

1989 In the early years of the Castlefield Carnival, Liverpool Road was closed to traffic and stalls and displays were set up along the pavements. This display was organised by the National Museum of Labour History and is outside the Air and Space Gallery of the Museum of Science and Industry, which was a former market hall. The carnival provides a novel way of attracting people and engaging their interest in organisations and places they might not have come across before or would not ordinarily been interested in.

1989 One area which has changed dramatically in the last 20 years has been Castlefield, created as Britain's first Urban Heritage Park in the early 1980s. As well as being the site of the Roman fort, the North Gate of which has been reconstructed, it was also the Manchester terminus of the Bridgewater and Rochdale Canals and of the Liverpool & Manchester Railway, and was crossed by a series of railway viaducts dating from the 1840s, 1870s and 1890s. Work on cleaning up the area and making it attractive to visitors started around 1980 and is an ongoing project. This photograph was taken in 1988 at the Inland Waterways National Rally, which was held shortly after the arms had been cleared of rubbish.

1992 Throughout the summer months a number of events are held in Castlefield. In 1992, it was the location for a European Markets Festival whereby market traders from many parts of Europe were invited to come to Manchester to display and sell traditional products from their home country. Dominating the scene is the viaduct which formerly carried the railway lines into the Great Northern Railway goods warehouse. Many of the events held here in the late 1980s and early '90s were in support of Manchester's bid to host the Olympic Games.

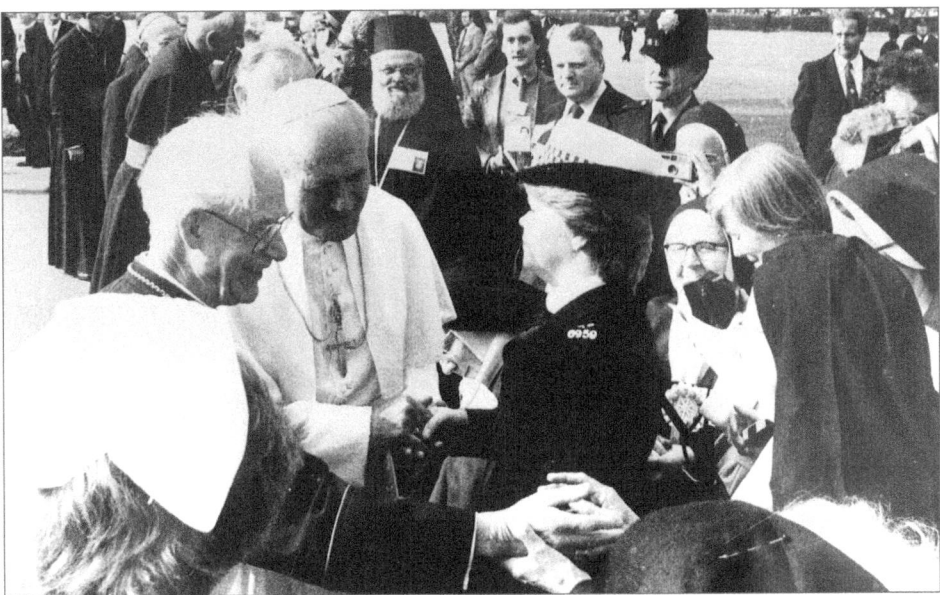

1982 In 1982, Pope John Paul visited England and celebrated mass on a number of occasions before huge crowds. In Manchester, the venue for the mass was Heaton Park, which was attended by people from all over the area. So huge were the numbers involved that special transport arrangements had to be laid on to get people to and from the event. Here the Pope, accompanied by the Bishop of Salford, is seen speaking to a member of the Greater Manchester Police Force on duty at Heaton Park, while in the background is a priest from one of the Orthodox churches and the Archbishop of Westminster, Cardinal Basil Hume.

1993 During the past 15 years, Manchester has mounted three bids to stage major international sporting events, the 1996 and 2000 Olympics and the 2002 Commonwealth Games, of which only the latter has been successful. The bid which appears to have attracted the most interest and enthusiasm was that for the 2000 Olympic Games. On the day of the announcement of the successful bidder, a large crowd gathered at the Castlefield Arena, next to the Staffordshire arm of the Bridgewater Canal, to await the news. Unfortunately, Manchester was not successful, but this did not stop Mancunians having a party which went on well into the evening.

1984 When the Manchester Science Museum was established, it was located in temporary premises which rapidly became too small. When Liverpool Road Station became available, it was decided to convert the station and three of the warehouses into a new home for the museum. The first section to be opened was the Power Hall in the 1858 warehouse and gradually, as other buildings were restored, the site was opened up and the number of exhibits increased. In addition, the former City Hall, built as a market in the 1870s, and converted into an Air and Space Museum, and later incorporated into the Science Museum.

1996 In May 1994, a former hydraulic pumping station on the banks of the River Irwell in Manchester was opened as the PumpHouse Peoples History Museum which aimed to 'celebrate the lives of ordinary people at work, at home and at leisure, over the last 200 years' as well as provide a place where the National Museum of Labour History could display some of its unique collection of artefacts. This is one of the displays, a reconstruction of the kitchen of one of the suffragette leaders, Hannah Mitchell.

1997 The city has always been an important centre for research in both the arts and sciences. The resources held in the older libraries, such as Chetham's Library, Manchester Central Library and the John Rylands University Library, have been enhanced in recent years by the collections held by organisations such as the National Museum of Labour History, the Working Class Movement Library in Salford, the Documentary Photographic Archive and the North West Film Archive. In 1997 Gordon Brown (Chancellor of the Exchequer) visited the Museum of Labour History to open a new reading room, after which he toured the building. Here he is seen inspecting some of the trade union banners which the museum has collected and restored.

1980 When the first houses were built in Wythenshawe, there were few facilities for its residents, but gradually these were built including a large lending and reference library, which also included a special children's library, seen here. The Forum complex also included a theatre, which with the library attracts readers and patrons from Stockport and Trafford as well as those who live in the area.

1984 Another facility which was provided for residents of Wythenshawe and those who worked there was a market hall and open-air market, close to the Forum and Birtles Adult Education Centre. The open-air section of the market appears to be well patronised if this illustration is any guide.

1999 When Central station was closed in 1969, it was over a decade before any positive suggestions were made as to its future. Eventually, the building was purchased by a company formed by the Greater Manchester County Council and an insurance company and plans were made to convert it into a much-needed exhibition centre in the heart of Manchester. Work was completed early in 1986 and the building opened just before the Greater Manchester Council was abolished. Known as G-Mex, the former railway station can be used as for both large and small exhibitions as well as for concerts and rallies.

1999 When Manchester's last tram ran in 1949, few expected ever to see trams running through the streets again. However, in 1991, work was completed on a rapid light transit system. known as Metrolink, which not only linked Piccadilly and Victoria stations on track laid through the streets, but also linked Bury and Altrincham, two towns on opposite sides of the city, by using existing railway lines. The tramway was opened by Elizabeth II on 17 July 1992 and soon became a great success, as it reduced some of the congestion between Manchester and the two towns it linked. Here one of the two-car trams, in street running mode, passes the former Central station. Work is now under way extending the system to Eccles via Salford Quays, and approval for further extensions is awaited.

1999 At the end of the Second World War, one of Manchester's priorities was to rebuild the Free Trade Hall, of which only the Peter Street and Southmill Street façades were standing. Although it involved fighting government restrictions on building materials, the hall was rebuilt and opened by Princess Elizabeth in 1951. Since its reopening, the Free Trade Hall has been used by the Hallé Orchestra as well as for concerts, meetings, speech days and some sporting events. The opening of the Bridgewater Hall in 1997 meant that the Free Trade Hall became redundant, and so far no new use has been found for this important historic building.

1999 Until the opening of the Bridgewater Hall in 1997, Manchester had never had a purpose-built concert hall, although there had been calls for one going back to the nineteenth century when Sir Charles Hallé suggested one should be built. It was not until the late 1980s that the idea of building a concert hall was given serious consideration and a suitable location found on Lower Mosley Street, on the site of the former bus station, and adjacent to the former Manchester and Salford Junction Canal, an arm of which was excavated to allow access to the hall for patrons wishing to arrive by boat. Although it is the home of Manchester's Hallé Orchestra, it is also used by other orchestras as well as for speech days and degree ceremonies.

115

1999 In 1972, a fire seriously damaged part of the former Merchants Warehouse, built in about 1825, on Castle Street. For over 20 years the building stood empty, but during the mid-1990s, work started on its restoration and conversion into offices. This has been very successful. Much of the improvement in the area around the Merchants Warehouse and across the road at the Duke 92 pub has been due to the energy of a local man, Jim Ramsbottom, who believed in the regeneration of the area.

1999 When Albert Square was created in the 1860s, the area where the statues and Albert Memorial were located was little more than a roundabout with traffic passing on all sides. Gradually, the width of the road in front of the Town Hall was reduced and in 1968, to mark the centenary of its establishment, the *Manchester Evening News* planted trees, which enhanced the area's appearance. During 1976–7, the Albert Memorial was restored for the first time since the restoration of 1894 for Queen Victoria's visit to open the Manchester Ship Canal. Eventually, traffic was stopped from passing in front of the Town Hall and the area was paved. The latest feature to be added to Albert Square is the fountain that had originally stood there to commemorate both the opening of the Thirlmere Aqueduct and Queen Victoria's Diamond Jubilee.

***c.* 1986** Manchester has one of the largest Chinese populations in the UK with the area around George Street having a large concentration of Chinese restaurants and shops. The area is officially known as China Town and even some of the street names are in English and Chinese. The most important feature of the area is this impressive Chinese Arch, one of only two outside China, constructed using traditional Chinese methods and materials.

1999 During the 1980s, British Rail gradually transferred the services which ran between Liverpool, Manchester, Yorkshire and the north-east and Scotland to Piccadilly station, leaving Victoria station under-used. An opportunity arose whereby part of the station was closed and a large arena, capable of holding over 17,000 spectators, was built together with a cinema and associated parking facilities. The Manchester Evening News Arena, as it is now known, is used for all types of musical events, sports events and rallies. It is home to the Manchester Storm ice hockey team and the Manchester Giants basketball side. Both teams are among the best in the country and have built up a large following. This view shows the approach to the arena across Hunts Bank.

1999 One of the largest covered shopping areas in Europe is the Arndale Centre, which covers some 15 acres and includes over 230 shops and stores. In addition, offices were provided in the tower block together with some residential accommodation. The first phase of the building was completed in 1972 and the final phase in 1995, but the IRA bomb of 1996 resulted in extensive damage to the Corporation Street end of the building, which is now being repaired and gradually reopened.

1999 For much of the twentieth century, the corner of Withy Grove and Shudehill was occupied by newspaper offices. Originally established by Edward Hulton, he sold the titles, offices and printing works to Allied Newspapers, later Kemsley Newspapers. It was here that the *Manchester Evening Chronicle*, *Sporting Chronicle* and *Athletic News* were published. With the contraction of the newspaper industry and changing methods of production, the building became redundant and is now to be included in a large leisure complex. While building work is going on, these attractive hoardings have been used to attract the interest of the general public.

1996 On the morning of 16 June 1996, the centre of Manchester was rocked by a loud explosion, the resultant blast of which severely damaged buildings over a wide area with the worst devastation being experienced along Corporation Street, Market Street, Cross Street and Cateaton Street. This photograph taken shortly after the blast shows the full extent of the devastation with panels on the Arndale Centre ripped out and Marks & Spencer's shop wrecked. Although there were injuries caused by flying glass and debris, no one was killed.

1996 A few days after the IRA bomb blast, police have finished their forensic examination of the site and workmen move in to make buildings safe while the future of the area is decided.

119

1999   One result of the bomb blast was that the opportunity was taken to re-plan and redevelop the area between St Mary's Gate/Market Street, Corporation Street, Fennel Street and Deansgate. This involved physically moving the Wellington Inn and Sinclairs Oyster Bar from their original location in the Market Place to a new site adjacent to the Mitre Hotel on Cateaton Street. Marks & Spencer's store is being rebuilt and the area receiving a major refurbishment and enhancement with increased pedestrianisation. Here the Wellington Inn is in its new location but the rest of the area is still a large building site.

1999   During May 1999, the world of English club football witnessed the achievement of what has been described as a unique treble – the Premier League Championship, the FA Cup and the European Cup – all won by a single club: Manchester United. Although Manchester United's ground is in Stretford, when the club returned home from Barcelona after their third success of the month, it was to Manchester that they came to be greeted by crowds estimated to be in the region of 750,000 people.

120

Acknowledgements and Picture Credits

Compiling this selection of illustrations to show Manchester in the twentieth century has been a challenge as so much material survives and so many different things have happened during the century. With a limited amount of space it has only been possible to show some of the events which took place, some of the scenes which have changed and some of the many asepcts of life in Manchester. Each section could fill a book on its own. My task has been made easier by the help I have received from many people. I would like thank all those who have helped in any way whatsoever either by lending photographs or providing information. In particular, I would like to thank Dr M. Powell of Chetham's Library, Alain Kahan of the Working Class Movement Library, Phil Dunn of the National Museum of Labour History, Bernard Champness, John Fletcher, George Turnbull of the Greater Manchester Transport Museum and Wythenshawe Library, David L. Jones of the Barbirolli Society, Alice Badjan and Richard Johnson of Aerofilms, David Taylor of Manchester Local Studies Unit, Neal Hyde of Hyde's Brewery and Lorna Balmforth from Castlefield Visitor Centre, the Royal Exchange Theatre Co, Joel Chester Fildes, Paul Catcheside, Director of Libraries and Theatres in Manchester, Mark Broady of the Greater Manchester Police Museum and the Archives Department of the Museum of Science and Industry in Manchester. I would also like to thank Suttons for asking me to compile this book and all those who have taken and preserved photographs from the past without which such books would not be possible.

I would also like to thank the following people and organisations for permission to reproduce some of the photographs in this book: Science Museum in Manchester, National Museum of Labour History, Working Class Movement Library, Manchester Public Libraries Local Studies Department and Wythenshawe Library, Manchester City Engineers Department, Chetham's Library, Aerofilms, Joel Chester Fildes, Manchester Literary and Philosophical Society, Greater Manchester Transport Museum Society and Greater Manchester Police Museum. Although I have tried to trace the owners of all those illustrations which required permission to reproduce, there are several for which there is no indication of their ownership. I apologise for any infringement of copyright that might have occurred as a result of this failure and hope that the owners will accept this apology.

Special thanks must be given to David Brearley who has made copies of photographs for this book together with the new ones for modern Manchester. Without David's help and assistance many of the illustrations in this book could not have been included. I must also thank Peter and Anna for their help and assistance and finally my wife, Hilary, for her help in reading drafts and making suggestions.

Thank you, everyone who has helped. Without your help, this book would not have been possible.

This book was first published in 1999 by Sutton Publishing Limited

This new paperback edition first published in 2007 by Sutton Publishing.

Reprinted in 2009 by
The History Press
The Mill, Brimscombe Port,
Stroud, Gloucestershire, GL5 2QG
www.thehistorypress.co.uk

Reprinted 2010, 2011, 2012, 2013

British Library Cataloguing in Publication Data
A catalogue record for this book is available from the British Library.

ISBN 978-0-7509-4917-0

Front endpaper: The offices of the *Manchester Guardian*, 1902.
Back endpaper: Although Manchester can trace its origins back to the Roman occupation of the area, modern Manchester is the product of the last two and a half centuries. The old market town was substantially rebuilt in the nineteenth century and many of these buildings have been replaced in the latter half of the twentieth century. Yet pockets of these earlier buildings remain, such as one side of Market Street where, facing the Arndale Centre, stand buildings from the nineteenth century. All that is required is for people to use their eyes and look above shop windows. It is surprising what remains in 1999.
Half title page: These children are waiting for the arrival of the special train which was to take them into the country, away from the threat posed by German air raids, 1939.
Title page: The bookstall at Victoria station, operated by W.H. Smith & Son, 1908.

Typeset in Photina.
Typesetting and origination by
Sutton Publishing.
Printed and bound in England.

c. **1910** An elderly gentleman feeds the pigeons at the base of the Albert Memorial.